Professional Development for Teachers

# Teaching and Assessing Skills in
# Foreign Languages

Caroline Woods

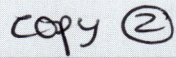

CAMBRIDGE
UNIVERSITY PRESS

CAMBRIDGE UNIVERSITY PRESS
Cambridge, New York, Melbourne, Madrid, Cape Town, Singapore, São Paulo

Cambridge University Press
The Edinburgh Building, Cambridge CB2 2RU, UK

www.cambridge.org
Information on this title: www.cambridge.org/9780521601030

© University of Cambridge International Examinations 2005

First published 2005

Printed in the United Kingdom at the University Press, Cambridge

*A catalogue record for this publication is available from the British Library*

ISBN-13   978-0-521-60103-0 paperback
ISBN-10   0-521-60103-7 paperback

# Contents

# Foreword

Teaching is a complex and demanding profession. All over the world, societies change in response to new knowledge gained, technological developments, globalisation and a requirement for an ever-more sophisticated and educated population. Teachers are in the forefront of such social change, responding with speed and confidence to the new demands made of them, in terms of both their knowledge and the way in which they teach. This series is intended to help them in their adaptation to change and in their professional development as teachers.

Curriculum changes worldwide are putting increased emphasis on the acquisition of skills as well as subject knowledge, so that students will have the ability to respond flexibly to the swiftly changing modern environment. As a result, teachers must be able both to teach and assess skills and to adjust their own teaching methods to embrace a wider range of techniques for both teaching and assessing in the classroom. The books in this series are practical handbooks which explore these techniques and offer advice on how to use them to enhance the teacher's own practice.

The handbooks are written by teachers with direct experience of teaching and assessing skills at this level. We have asked them to write for their readers in such a way that the readers feel directly supported in their professional development. Thus, there are tasks for teachers, pauses for reflection and questions to be answered. We hope that readers will find that this mixture of the practical and the professional helps them, both in their practice and in their own sense of what it means to be an effective teacher in this modern, changing world of international education.

Dr Kate Pretty
Series Editor

# 1 Introduction
# Purpose and context – an overview

This book is aimed at teachers throughout the world involved in teaching Foreign Languages (FL). It will be applicable to teachers preparing students for examinations in FL through programmes like the University of Cambridge International Examinations (CIE) IGCSE, O Level, GCSE and the International Baccalaureate Middle Years, but the CIE IGCSE syllabus for FL is used as the exemplar throughout this book.

This first chapter sets out the content and aims of the book and reflects upon the importance of FL learning. Chapter 2 sets out possible approaches to interpreting a syllabus and planning a programme of study. Chapter 3 reflects upon methodology and key issues in FL teaching such as the use of the Target Language (TL) in the classroom. This chapter also includes a section on formative assessment. Chapters 4–7 are concerned with the skills of Listening, Speaking, Reading and Writing. Each of these chapters starts with some theoretical background and discussion, and moves on to relate assessment objectives to teaching objectives within the classroom context. Finally, Chapter 8 gives an overview of ICT in FL teaching.

Teaching FL is, without doubt, challenging and rewarding. In the past 20 years or so, language teaching methodologies have evolved and examinations have reflected these changes. These changes have had a great impact on the learning experience of our students and, as teachers, we have had to adapt and evolve so as to meet our students' needs.

As FL teachers we have had to choose effective and appropriate methods to develop knowledge about, and skills in, the TL with students. Within the international context this may be particularly challenging. The local learning environment may be several thousand miles removed from a country where the TL is spoken, and the local learning context and financial constraints may influence the approach and methodology within schools. Different mother-tongue cultures may place more or less importance on the need to acquire a foreign language, and this can have consequences in terms of attitudes and motivation towards the TL in our learners. Likewise, certain cultural contexts may place more or less importance on perceived 'traditional methodology' or 'more modern methodology', and tensions sometimes arise over the balance between the perceived importance of Reading/Writing and Speaking/Listening skills.

For nearly 20 years I have taught within a European context and, as a Principal Examiner, I have trained teachers in many countries. It is very clear that no two international FL classrooms are the same. Firstly, the mix of learners is unique in *every* classroom. Secondly, the local context is different; classes may be large (35+ students) or small (2–3 students), in sets according to ability, or within very mixed-ability groups. Different economic factors at a local level can have huge implications for teaching time available, size of class and resourcing.

Different methodologies at the local level can also place a different emphasis on the use of the TL within the learning environment. Whatever the local context, the teacher remains the *most* important resource, who cannot be replaced by a coursebook or examination syllabus. As teachers, we remain the initial and most important exemplar of the TL to our students, which, in turn, can raise further questions concerning our approach to teaching our students. If classes have one common mother tongue and a teacher with the same mother tongue, it can sometimes be expedient to use the mother tongue in terms of time (e.g. when teaching a grammar point). If teachers operate in an English working environment with students of diverse mother-tongue languages, English may from time to time be appropriate. However, in a classroom of students who have different mother tongues from the teacher, this may not be the case. If we bear in mind all these different possible scenarios, we can arrive at a solution of 'optimum' use of the TL. Some teachers feel comfortable with this, but for others it can be a source of anxiety as there are implications in terms of classroom management. These issues will be examined later.

The role of assessment is also a critical area to be explored. Assessment can take several forms. Assessment carried out during the course of study can inform us about how well students are performing in the short term. It can help us to evaluate students' learning experiences, and inform us as to future targets and help us to plan courses and learning strategies (formative assessment). In the case of external examinations, such as IGCSE and O Level, assessment must provide a reliable end-of-course measurement of what candidates have achieved (summative assessment). It is crucial, therefore, to explore the aims and assessment objectives of such examinations and to think to what extent the learning process reflects and complements these aims and objectives. Do we teach too closely to examinations, or do we stray too far? The relationship between examinations and learning content needs careful evaluation. To what extent can we make these two elements complementary?

Examinations are often intended to test separate skills (e.g. Speaking or Listening), but even if the end result is expressed in terms of a single skill the processes involved in testing may require more than one language skill. In Speaking, the Listening skill is vital; and in Listening, candidates make use of both Reading and Writing skills in order to answer questions, even if these are not formally assessed. It is assumed that, likewise in the classroom, the skills of Listening, Speaking, Reading and Writing are integrated. This issue will be explored – though, for ease of use, the assessment and teaching of each of the different skills are treated separately in this book.

This book is written *not* with the aim of prescribing particular methodologies or advocating learning strategies and programmes conceived merely to fulfil examination requirements; it is intended to stimulate the reader in their local situation to reflect on their own personal teaching style and approach, to take stock and develop their own style if and where necessary. There may be new areas to explore, or ones to consolidate. It is hoped that the tips and reflective activities will help such exploration and provide some useful pointers for further fruitful activities.

## Why study a foreign language?

It can be a very interesting exercise to ask new FL learners why they think that they are learning another language. Most of my new learners cite the following:

- It is useful on holiday!
- We 'have' to!
- I may be able to work abroad in the future.
- It will be fun and/or interesting.

The same question asked of 16-year-olds about to face their final examinations yields more:

- I have learnt about life in another country and realised that different habits and customs are not bad or good, just different.
- I can communicate with people abroad and when I'm older I may be able to live or work abroad. It has helped me to make friends abroad.
- I think I will be able to pick up another foreign language because I have learnt one already.
- It's been hard work, but I have enjoyed the challenge.
- It's been different from anything else at school.

These students' responses encapsulate – in an honest, though perhaps not very sophisticated, way – much of what is important in the aims of FL learning. In today's world, languages are one of the few things that bring people together. Linguists frequently display tolerance and understanding. Languages bring together rather than divide. They encourage integration and communication, and give learners greater insight into the culture and civilisation of areas where the language is spoken. Many teachers I have met in international schools talk of the vital role of their subject in encouraging positive attitudes towards speakers of foreign languages and a sympathetic approach to foreign cultures. Many of our students, especially in the context of international schools, will live and work abroad, and indeed will already be studying in a country other than the country of their birth. Foreign languages will (and may already) be a vital part of their successful integration in another country. Employers worldwide value languages highly; the ability to work and communicate in a language other than English can open up opportunities to students in all areas of employment.

Learning a foreign language complements other areas of a student's learning experience by encouraging skills of a more general application, such as memorising and analysis. This is indeed one of the aims cited by the CIE IGCSE syllabus for FL, which also highlights another aim which goes beyond the utilitarian: that of providing enjoyment and intellectual stimulation. It is valuable to students to be challenged to think and learn in ways that are different from those they experience in other areas of the school curriculum. It is even better if they can enjoy the process, as learning a language can, quite simply, be good fun and very satisfying. As one student said, it can also make learning another language easier, as language learning skills are frequently transferable.

Not all our students will continue their study of a language beyond four or five years, and some will find it harder than others. But, at the least, many will have acquired new study skills and a positive appreciation of another language and the countries where the language is spoken. These are all life-enhancing attributes that help educate our students to be world citizens.

# 2 Interpreting the syllabus and planning a programme of study

It is crucial to have a well-planned scheme of work and to use materials to deliver your lessons that ensure full coverage of the examination syllabus.

This chapter considers how best to plan a programme of study and choose teaching and learning materials which will ensure appropriate coverage of the syllabus. The syllabus used as an example is the CIE IGCSE syllabus for Foreign Languages (FL).

## Understanding the syllabus

All syllabuses will provide certain information, but this may be organised in different ways. The CIE IGCSE syllabus for FL has four main sections: aims, assessment objectives, assessment, and curriculum content. These sections provide detail on what needs to be taught and how it is assessed.

## Aims

The aims of the syllabus describe the educational purposes of a course in a foreign language (Chapter 1 discussed these aims).

## Assessment objectives

The assessment objectives describe the skills that are assessed in the examination papers. For the CIE IGCSE syllabus in FL the one assessment objective is Communication, which incorporates four subskills, as follows:

- A Listening
- B Speaking
- C Reading
- D Writing

Clearly these are interlinked, and for each component of the examination a variety of skills may be needed. For example, Speaking, Listening and Reading skills will all be needed for Paper 3, Speaking; but the actual marks awarded will be for the candidate's ability to produce spoken foreign language.

## Assessment

This section describes the scheme of assessment and explains how it works. Focusing on the CIE IGCSE syllabus for FL, we can see that there are two levels of assessment: the Core Curriculum for less able students, and the Extended Curriculum for more able students. We can also see what the implications are of choosing one level or the other. For example, if students prepare the Core Curriculum and are entered for the Core Curriculum papers, they have access only to grades C to G, while if they prepare the Extended Curriculum and are entered for the Extended Curriculum papers, the full range of grades A* to G is available to them. Another important point to note when considering a scheme of assessment is the relative weighting accorded to the separate skills. In the CIE IGCSE syllabus for FL each of the skills makes an equal contribution to the final examination grade. As one delegate said to me recently on a training session, this has implications for teachers in terms of planning a programme of study. If all the skills are equally important, then a well-planned programme will need to allow for regular practice and use of all skills in the classroom. This may sound a little obvious, but it would be totally inappropriate to base a teaching programme entirely on Reading and Writing skills if the assessment framework requires competence in all four skills. This, in turn, will affect our choice of teaching and learning materials.

The assessment section of the CIE IGCSE syllabus for FL includes a description of the examination papers. Such descriptions are best viewed alongside past examination papers (a sample of which, in the case of CIE IGCSE, are available online at www.cie.org.uk via the link on the Home page to Syllabuses). A detailed explanation is also provided of what marks are available for each section of the examination papers. There is a description of the question types used in exercises and the kind of sources which occur in the papers. Again, this kind of information can assist when choosing coursebooks and teaching materials. Guidance is also given as to how marks are awarded by examiners. The example below is taken from the Paper 2, Reading and Directed Writing, description:

The Reading exercises are designed to test comprehension skills. If the candidate clearly communicates the message, the mark indicated in the bracket alongside the question is scored. This means that a candidate s written work may be less than accurate and still gain the mark. If, however, the language used is so inaccurate as to make the message ambiguous, the mark is not awarded.

This further example of the approach taken to the awarding of marks is taken from the Paper 4, Continuous Writing, description:

> Candidates are expected to communicate as accurately as possible, and should, in so doing, make use of a wider variety of idiom, vocabulary, structure and appropriate tense. A system of positive marking is used to assess the written tasks. The system rewards qualities and merit rather than penalising shortcomings. Examiners seek material worthy of credit and do not indicate errors.

Both the above examples underline the positive approach underpinning the assessment framework of the CIE IGCSE syllabus in FL and emphasise the way in which candidates are rewarded for what they know and can do, rather than penalised for what they cannot do. Again, it is important to bear in mind the approach to assessment of your chosen syllabus, and the way in which examiners will award marks, when deciding upon materials and teaching/learning strategies in class.

## Curriculum content

In the curriculum content section of the CIE IGCSE syllabus for FL, teachers will find outlined the skills and subject content to be assessed in the examination. In terms of planning a programme of study, the curriculum content is vital. FL teachers need to know the expectations of the examiners in terms of both grammatical knowledge and topics. In most cases, the CIE IGCSE syllabus will include a list of topics, split into five areas:

- Area A Everyday activities
- Area B Personal and social life
- Area C The world around us
- Area D The world of work
- Area E The international world

The purpose of the topic list is to provide a manageable content which offers teachers flexibility in the planning of their courses, but places restrictions on the topic areas from which examiners may make their choice of texts.

In addition, for most individual CIE IGCSE FL syllabuses there exists alongside the syllabus document an invaluable publication called the *Defined Content* booklet. We shall consider below how such a document can aid our planning and inform our evaluation of materials.

- Study the syllabus and past examination papers for your subject. Match up the paper description to past examination papers.
- Is the scheme of assessment differentiated? Note what the expectations are for a Core Curriculum candidate and an Extended Curriculum candidate.
- Try to relate the demands of the syllabus to your own teaching groups and evaluate the extent to which your present teaching programme matches up to these expectations.
- Is your present teaching approach a reflection of what is being assessed in this framework, or are there certain skills that may be under- or over-represented?

## *Defined Content* booklets

The *Defined Content* booklets are an invaluable resource when planning a programme of study and converting a syllabus into a scheme of work.

The CIE IGCSE FL *Defined Content* booklets outline five main **topic areas** and then go on to provide a **minimum core vocabulary** list for Topic Areas A, B and C and further indications of study for Topic Areas D and E. This information is best used as a checklist against which you should consider your teaching materials and schemes of work. It is essential to cross-map the content of your coursebook and teaching materials against the booklet to check that the topics and vocabulary which students will need in the examination are all covered in your chosen programme.

Also included is a list of examination rubrics (instructions) which candidates will encounter on the different examination papers. This list should form part of your teaching programme, and candidates should feel at ease with these instructions – they are not meant to be part of the test – as they are a way into the questions. Candidates should see these and learn them well in advance of the examination.

The final part of the booklet gives a clear list of structures and grammar. The list indicates the grammatical knowledge required in different sections of the examination. Again, this list should be checked against your coursebook and teaching materials.

## Choosing teaching materials

If you are new to the examination and just planning a programme of study, it may seem daunting. The following guidelines will be of use:

- Familiarise yourself with your chosen syllabus (as outlined above).
- Ensure you are aware of any resources provided by the examination board to support the syllabus. These may be available in a publications catalogue or online.

- Often examination boards will provide a list of published materials (from a variety of publishers) which are deemed appropriate for a particular syllabus. It cannot be stressed enough that different students in different countries will have different requirements, owing to previous learning experiences. The time allotted to an FL programme of study may also vary dramatically from country to country. Any resource lists provided are not intended to be exhaustive. An examination such as CIE IGCSE is taken in a large number of countries, and teachers may well be using, or considering, local coursebooks not included on CIE resource lists. This does not mean they are inappropriate for your students – but you will need to map your own local resources against your chosen syllabus and assess the extent to which all skills are covered.
- Evaluate your students' needs against the *Defined Content* booklet where applicable and, especially if money is short, consider purchasing half-sets of a good coursebook and a separate skills practice handbook if your students need practice in one particular skill.
- Consider the approach of the coursebook carefully. Bearing in mind the requirements of your chosen syllabus, does the coursebook give adequate practice in the four skills? Does the course content reflect the topics and grammar you need to teach? If the coursebook is entirely in the Target Language (TL), are the exercises accessible? Do they match up to the test types used in the examination papers your students will be sitting?
- Consider the supporting materials (such as workbooks and worksheets) and visual aids available for each coursebook. Some not only have flashcards, overhead transparencies and audio cassettes, but are now also appearing with DVD- and CD-based supporting materials.
- Consider the assessment programme of a coursebook. Does it provide testing points / stages that will enable you to evaluate how well your students are progressing?

Once you are familiar with the syllabus and have identified appropriate materials, it is important to break down the syllabus and study programme into manageable chunks. Most coursebooks now approach their content coverage via topics, with a linguistic progression within these topics and from topic to topic. In the case of the CIE IGCSE syllabus for FL, for example, you are free to choose the order in which you cover topics and this, coupled with a good coursebook, provides great flexibility. But, do remember that no one coursebook is likely to be the perfect match to a syllabus. Learners' needs will vary enormously in different contexts. I usually work to the topic order as presented in the coursebook as this ensures linguistic progression. But I feel free to veer away from the book and supplement sections, or miss out other sections, when necessary.

## Scheme of work

The scheme of work I use (which has been pre-mapped against examination requirements) is not merely a list of topics and structures covered in the coursebook. It also includes learning aims and objectives in terms of tasks for each skill, and there are opportunities to carry out formative testing at the end of each unit of work so that this feedback can inform my planning. Within each unit of the scheme of work, there is a final section entitled 'Learning activities', which can be used for the more detailed content of individual lesson plans. This in turn is linked to resources available for such activities.

## Lesson plans

Once your overall scheme of work is in place, your lesson plans need to be developed.

For each lesson, consider the following:

- The objectives of the lesson (write these up on the board so that students know what is to be covered).
- A 'starter' activity which links back to previous work covered or which looks forward to the lesson content. Ideally, this needs to be an activity that will get the students involved.
- How the lesson / learning content will be covered. This usually includes at least two skills and I am unlikely to rely solely on the coursebook as a resource. A variety of learning strategies should be incorporated which, if possible, involve not just teacher–student contact, but also student–student contact. I try to ensure that for each skill there is a main activity for all to cover and extension materials for the more able students.
- A recall session at the end. It is important to make the students aware both that the lesson objectives have been covered and of what they have actually achieved.

It is also important to consider the timings of the lesson and of the homework follow-up activities that review the lesson content and give the possibility of further extension work. The key to any successful lesson is pace and progression, and it is useful to think of timings when planning. A lesson plan which takes into account the above factors enables pace and progression to be apparent – not just to the teacher, but also to the learner.

## Teacher activity 2.2

Draw up a lesson plan on the topic of holidays (the lesson content to be delivered should be based on eliciting an account – oral or written – in the perfect tense of a recent trip).

Include the objectives of the lesson, a starter activity, the lesson content and activities and how you will deliver it (teaching method). Consider the timings, resources required and student activities. Also include a final recap session. Consider an appropriate homework activity to reinforce the learning.

## LOOKING BACK

- ◆ How far might your understanding of the aims and assessment objectives of your syllabus affect your classroom teaching?
- ◆ To what extent do your schemes of work match the requirements of the assessment objectives?
- ◆ How far does your teaching/learning programme match the curriculum content of your chosen examination?
- ◆ Consider your lesson plans. Are there certain skills that you do not regularly practise?

# 3 Key issues in teaching and assessing Foreign Languages

In this chapter we shall examine key current issues, such as where we are in terms of methodology, the notion of authenticity, teaching and assessing in the Target Language (TL), and formative assessment.

## Where are we in terms of methodology?

From the late 1970s, methodology moved away from a grammar–translation approach, which emphasised describing the language rather than using it. This was also reflected in a change in testing methods: there was a move away from, for example, large-scale multiple-choice objective tests based on testing discrete items and traditional translation. As the methodology moved towards stressing the importance of the ability of the learner to perform in the TL, test designers were challenged to produce tests that could assess the extent to which learners could actually communicate in the TL.

As early as 1965, Chomsky had already made a fundamental distinction between **competence** (the speaker/hearer's knowledge of the language) and **performance** (the actual use of language in concrete situations). Hymes (1972) added the notion of **communicative** to competence – and this meant adding rules of use of language without which the rules of grammar would be useless.

Bachman (1990) referred to communicative language ability. This comprised two main forms of competence: linguistic competence and pragmatic competence. Linguistic competence was knowledge of the language itself, defined in terms of pronunciation, vocabulary, grammar and sentence structure. Pragmatic competence was knowing *how* to use language to achieve communicative goals or intentions. It involved the use of social knowledge to select language forms to use in different settings.

The new emphasis in methodology was on the actual process of communication and how to teach learners to communicate. New teaching materials reflected this shift away from Reading/Writing to focus on more Speaking/Listening activities, which featured much greater use of the TL.

Grammar still had a place but it was considered less important than the acquisition of real-life communication skills and communicative ability.

The debate of recent years has largely centred on how to develop communicative language ability in our students. Brumfit (1984) talked of the need for activities to promote fluency. In his view, fluency activities enable students to produce and understand items which they gradually acquire during activities which are focused on linguistic form or 'accuracy work'. When considering fluency activities, he cited several factors to be borne in mind:

- What is the need of the learners? (To what use will the language be put?)
- Language is a means to an end – the focus should be on meaning, not form.
- Content should be determined by the learner, who is the speaker or writer.
- There must be negotiation of meaning between speakers – students are involved in interpreting a meaning from what they hear.
- There should be unpredictable language – as there is in real life – with an information gap (a gap of understanding that can only be bridged by real communication).
- The normal processes of listening, reading, speaking and writing are in play (e.g. improvisation, paraphrasing).
- Teacher intervention should be minimal.

Such activities and emerging research in the field of linguistics and language acquisition led to heated debate about the best ways forward in terms of methodology. One prevailing misconception was the idea that accuracy and grammar were no longer important. Teachers and producers of textbooks became preoccupied with how best to integrate input on language form, rehearsal and communicative practice. Teachers found it difficult to reproduce real-life situations in the classroom and to control language in real communicative situations.

The biggest criticism that could perhaps be aimed at the methodology of the 1990s was that much syllabus development and coursebook development focused heavily on topic-based teaching which ignored, or paid little attention to, a sound linear development in terms of structure, vocabulary and grammar. This led to many learners acquiring 'phrasebook knowledge' and a marked inability to transfer their language skills between topics. Syllabuses were developed around speech acts, and these generally placed far less emphasis on grammar, marginalising it in the learning process. This was particularly the case where the whole ability range was learning the foreign language. The desire to motivate sometimes unwilling learners often led to attractive-looking coursebooks with little linguistic content and a topic-based approach, which never enabled students to move beyond a very basic level of language acquisition.

The move towards a communicative language teaching (CLT) methodology led away from the overemphasis on Writing as the traditionally all-important language skill. Teaching and testing focused upon the equal importance of skills, but frequently at the expense of a sound framework of grammar – even for learners for whom it was entirely appropriate to emphasise not just communicative but also linguistic competence. More able learners sometimes became frustrated that they were not being given the means to generate new language. Phrases and lists of vocabulary alone were not enough to help learners acquire strategies for coping in real life. Unfortunately, the emphasis on communicative competence sometimes failed to take into account the complementary nature of linguistic competence.

## So, where are we now?

It is fair to say, at the time of writing, that communication is still at the heart of language teaching methodology, but that grammar has re-emerged. It is now deemed quite acceptable and, indeed, desirable practice to make the linguistic content of our teaching very obvious to students. Grammar and accuracy are once again seen as important. Schemes of work and lesson plans now have to place greater emphasis on helping students to write and speak more accurately, and to understand how linguistic principles work and are applied in Reading and Listening texts. This does not mean that Writing is re-emerging as the most important of the four subskills. It does, however, mean that, whereas many teachers in the 1990s may have felt that teaching grammar was frowned upon, it is being re-established as an important and vital feature of language acquisition and use. This is already apparent in the way new publications have responded and made their grammatical content much more explicit. It is heartening to note that, in many of the countries where I have met international teachers, the concept of teaching grammar was always seen to be one aspect of communication. Such teachers have continued to emphasise the acquisition of structures and accuracy in their own classrooms, alongside a communicative approach. This approach is an entirely sensible one and one which will not be alien to many reading this publication.

- To what extent did your own experience as a foreign language learner reflect aspects of linguistic competence and aspects of communicative competence?
- Consider your basic approach in the classroom. Does your own teaching style reflect a communicative approach – and, if so, to what extent? What are the dangers or difficulties of adopting a totally communicative approach in your own context?

## Authenticity

Closely tied in to the notion of CLT was the notion of authenticity. Authenticity became a paramount objective, both in terms of the nature of task (that it should totally reflect a real-life situation) and of text (that it should be an unchanged authentic foreign language text).

Authenticity of task required teachers and materials authors to produce clearly defined and real-life purposeful tasks. In theory, this was fine; but the notion of authenticity became somewhat removed when one considered that the students were *not* in real-life situations, neither in the classroom nor in the examination room. There is a certain step back to be taken in the teaching context and, however well-meaning the teacher is and however well-motivated the learner is, it is not always easy to achieve an authentic learning situation. As Pachler and Field (2002: 46) comment, there is a difference between 'learning a language for communication and learning it as communication'. Certain transactional situations such as buying tickets and ordering meals lend themselves to real-life situations. Once into the realm of freer language, it is very challenging to set up situations in which the tasks are authentic and will occur naturally, given that students have only a limited amount of linguistic competence upon which to draw. Teachers and authors therefore frequently fall back upon the authenticated task – in other words, setting up lifelike tasks which require a limited amount of controlled and pre-rehearsed language, which can be presented, practised and then developed in different situations.

In order to reflect the authenticity of text, the nature of examination tasks and coursebook materials changed. Students were presented with a huge variety of texts drawn from authentic materials. Initially, this appeared to be a totally laudable departure from previously encountered materials, but there were problems. Firstly, in the classroom learners are in an artificial situation. They are not immersed in the culture of the TL, and this can be a huge problem if the background knowledge brought to the text by the student is insufficient to comprehend the subject matter. Secondly, if the language is not adapted to match the learning objectives appropriate to the learner, the text may prove to be so inaccessible that the learner gives up and will not rise to the challenge. In practice, authors and teachers automatically filter the language to make it more accessible and appropriate to the linguistic level of students. Although this may go against the truly communicative approach of meeting unpredictable language in a real-life situation, it is a fact that for texts to have meaning they require teachers to make them relevant to their learners' needs. The teacher remains the best source of reference between the classroom and the outside world of the country where the TL is spoken, and has a vital role to play in filtering texts to make them appropriate to their students.

Test designers are well aware of the need to provide materials which look authentic and are based on authentic sources, but which contain language that is within the scope of the syllabus. This helps teachers to design programmes of study and also gives achievable teaching and assessment objectives – if there were no limits placed on an examination in terms of topic content, structures, vocabulary and grammar, then reliable assessment would be virtually impossible as the whole of human life could be there! It is necessary to be realistic in terms of what the average 16-year-old reads or hears in their own mother tongue and to consider their learning environment before plunging them into a totally 'authentic' language-learning experience.

In my own experience, it is always of paramount importance to consider the authenticity of task and text in relation to the pupils' needs. One can gradually grade both text and task in terms of difficulty of content and language as they progress. As the teacher in the local environment, *you* are the expert who can lead them from total dependence to a degree of coping with the unknown/unpredictable in an independent way, but this needs to be a structured process – one should not aim to present an authentic task or text with no preparation. Ways of preparing a task or text are suggested in the various skills chapters.

## Teaching in the Target Language

There are two distinct camps of international schools in terms of Foreign Language (FL) teaching. Firstly, there are those where the FL teachers have a truly international clientele composed of students with a variety of mother tongues – recourse to one 'explanatory tongue' is therefore not an option, and the TL may have to be used all the time. Secondly, there are schools where a language other than the FL being studied is the working language, and where one can expect students to understand explanations which are not in the FL but in the working language. Whatever the case, it is clear that communicative methodology has gone hand-in-hand with a pedagogical approach emphasising maximum use of the TL as both a teaching and a learning medium.

Within the UK context (where there has been much emphasis since the mid-1990s on maximum use of the TL by teachers), it is not always apparent that such maximum use by teachers has led to maximum use by students. International colleagues frequently tell me the same. We operate in classrooms where we demand a certain 'suspension of belief' by students – however many posters we display of the TL country. We also risk, it must be stated, a certain alienation on the part of our students in terms of motivation. Factors such as lesson length, resourcing and the teacher's confidence in their use of the TL can also play a vital role in the delivery of the lesson. So, where do we start? Different cultural contexts and pedagogical stances may put more or less emphasis on the delivery of a teaching programme entirely in the TL.

Perhaps, the most important questions to ask in your own context are these:
- What are the needs of my students?
- Do they have a common mother tongue or common working language other than the TL?
- Do I want to teach a whole lesson entirely in the FL? If not, how will students know which language to operate in?
- If I choose to operate entirely in the FL, how may this affect the class in terms of management? Will there be implications in terms of classroom control?
- Am I a native speaker, very able FL speaker or perhaps a less-than-confident FL speaker myself? (This has implications as native and FL speakers 'filter' language to learners in different ways.)

## Teacher activity 3.2

Make an approximate assessment of your FL activity in the class.
- To what extent do you use the TL?
- Is it effective and well planned?
- Do you switch between languages, or do you have clear periods of time for TL use?
- To what extent do you use the TL?
- To what extent do your students use the TL themselves?

## Why is it 'good' to teach in the foreign language?

Firstly, the number of different mother tongues in the teaching group may mean teachers have no choice. Secondly, there are sound pedagogical reasons. As teachers, we provide a model. Whatever the paucity or diversity of the teaching context, you remain the best model for FL use. Maximum use of the TL in class serves to give students a living model and can increase Listening skills immensely, but as Macaro (2000: 178) states, FL learners cannot pick up the FL like babies in the mother-tongue situation – the teaching in the TL needs to be **systematic** to be effective. We need to think very carefully about schemes of work and to what extent we introduce a variety of vocabulary and phrases in a regulated way, enabling students to react confidently in the FL situation. Macaro (2000: 179) hypothesises that learners use their own mother tongue to help them decode texts. For all but the most advanced learners, the mother tongue is seen as a primary source of comparison and contextualisation. The language of pure thought for many remains the mother tongue. We should learn to accept this reality, whilst trying to put forward a diversity of learning situations and strategies which afford our students maximum, expedient, use of the TL in situations that do not threaten or demotivate them.

Macaro (1997: 6) lists reasons for use/non-use of the TL by teachers as follows:

### Positive:

- the amount of language acquired subconsciously by students;
- the improvement in listening skills;
- exploitation of the medium leading to new teaching and learning strategies;
- showing how important it is to students to learn a new language;
- demonstrating how the language can be used to do things.

### Negative:
- TL for instructions can be time consuming;
- reaching a point where remaining in TL becomes counter-productive;
- teaching in the TL is tiring and the teacher becomes ineffective.

## How do I encourage good use of the Target Language in students?

If you are a mother-tongue speaker operating in a non-TL environment, then there are specific questions to be addressed. To what extent does your own training coincide/conflict with an FL-learning environment? As a mother-tongue speaker, you will need to filter your language and pitch it at an appropriate level in the classroom.

My own experience of teaching English in a French school proved to me early on in my career that I needed to be much more systematic and structured in the introduction and repetition of lexical items for things such as classroom commands. Frequently, my learners were bemused as I hailed them with a torrent of foreign language. I worked within a department where there was no common policy on use of the TL and a textbook was slavishly followed. These are not approaches I would advocate personally. In my overenthusiasm to surround my French students with the TL, I was giving them too much, too quickly, and not really considering how confusing it was for them.

Any move to a greater use of the TL in the classroom should be a gradual process leading to positive outcomes. It will be more realistic, and less demotivating to students, if the TL is used in a way that enables different learners to develop strategies to acquire, practise and use it. If they fear failure, students will not want to communicate in the TL. It is essential that the teacher establishes an atmosphere of trust and confidence with students right from the beginning, so that motivation remains high and a positive atmosphere prevails.

## Teacher activity 3.3

- Consider a recent lesson with any year group in which the students' motivation was good and the use of the TL was considerable, by *both* you and the students.
- Consider which strategies made this possible. Was the lesson closely structured, with a clear introduction and presentation of language, and a clear summing up? Were activities varied? Were students active / passive / working solo or in groups?
- Was the use of the TL by students of a transactional or a freer nature?
- Were all instructions given in the TL and understood?
- If a mixture of languages was used, how did students know which one to use and when?

## Possible ways forward to develop the use of the Target Language

The following ideas and suggestions should prove helpful.

### Departmental policy

Firstly, is there one? A good policy will define clearly for each year group what all students are expected to be able to say and to understand in the TL. Ideally, students will have lists in their exercise books and record cards to which they can refer and which they can tick off as they go. These lists can be learnt for homework and closely tied in to units of work. They can be stuck into the back of the students' books, and can include comments used in the department to annotate and grade work. An excellent source of such instructions exists in French, German, Spanish, Italian and Russian in MacDonald (1993). This book is a most useful starting point for developing use of the TL, and is a very practical publication. Schools are allowed to photocopy and use these lists and this can save you some hours.

---

### Teacher activity 3.4

- Devise a list of instructions / classroom commands appropriate for a group of first-year learners.
- Think of ways in which these can be practised/exploited in a fun way (e.g. games such as Simon Says, posters for the classroom wall) which will reinforce their use.
- Get a group of younger learners to design and put up a set of classroom instructions in the TL.

---

## Rewards

As an FL teacher, I firmly believe in rewarding achievement. Praise is absolutely crucial in the FL classroom. Smiles, body language and reinforcement motivate enormously. If students use the TL to you or each other, set up a merit system that can feed into a credit system (if your school has one). Alternatively, good use of the TL by students can be rewarded by departmental certificates that form part of a student's record of achievement in the wider school context. Even a simple 'thumbs-up' sign or 'Bravo!' can bring a smile to a student's face. At the younger end of the spectrum, a prize for the best effort of the week can be awarded. Prizes do not need to be big; it is the recognition that counts.

## Planning lessons – using the time constructively

Consider the activities that lead to maximum target use by students. Usually, it is some form of Speaking activity – often linked to a visual, aural or written stimulus. But it is well worth considering that, if lessons are long, concentration will fall dramatically after 20 or so minutes. Some of my lessons, owing to timetable constraints, have been up to 80 minutes long. This is a huge slab of time. An FL learner cannot keep up their concentration and be active or receptive to the TL for all that time unless they are exceptionally able. It is necessary to vary pace and activity so that students have active, receptive periods and 'testing' periods during which their brains can filter and sort any new language. I once had Swahili and Norwegian taster lessons in the TL for an hour. After the total immersion,

I was exhausted, and desperate not to be asked a question! When planning lessons, ensure that different skills are practised and that the language presented is visually supported (with flashcards or OHP). It is also well worth a 2–3-minute break if the lesson is long. Get students to change places, stretch or just do nothing. That can help restore motivation and good will. A pile of TL magazines or readers can be good time-fillers in such rest periods.

## Links

The links between different phases of a lesson and a change of activity are usually best done in the TL. A hand clap, your hand in the air (students then have to follow the action in silence), a quick *Levez-vous* (or equivalent) or just writing *Silence* on the board can all work well. With the attention caught, you are free to move on to the next phase. Everybody develops their own ways, but TL input for the links and instructions is crucial to reinforce TL use and understanding.

## Correcting students' oral work in the Target Language

Students worldwide have one common fear: losing face in front of their peers. We have a basic quandary. We need to give correct language models, but is it always appropriate to stop a student and 'correct' them? A lot depends on how this is done. Many international colleagues at training sessions have indicated that in speaking activities a lot depends on the ability and learning goals of the individual learner. A more advanced learner with more confidence will probably receive constructive correction well; a less able student may feel totally threatened.

On Day 1 with new learners, I tell them (before we even start any TL) that I love them to make mistakes and that they will all learn better if they make them! Oral mistakes of language can be rewarded with a nod and a statement and smile, such as *I've understood* (in the TL) – *Good*, and a correct version can be proffered to the whole group or the individual to repeat. Correction must be supportive and non-threatening if students are to maintain the desire to participate. It is not a matter of discipline but of the desire to help the student, and some students need this to be made very clear.

---

### Teacher activity 3.5

Consider how you correct students' oral work. Do you have a method? Do you correct different students in different ways?

## Code switching

Beware! If, as a teacher, you operate in two languages, students may be totally unaware of when you want them to use the TL or the other language. At the worst, discipline may break down completely. It is important to establish clear rules or signs that indicate with the minimum amount of disruption when students can or cannot use the TL.

I tell my own students that there are times when I expect maximum effort on their and my part to use the TL, such as whole-class presentations of new work, arrivals, departures, instructions, requests, role plays and so on. This obviously presupposes that one equips students with phrases in the TL such as 'How do I say . . . in French, Spanish . . . ?', 'Please can you help me?', 'I can't do this', 'I don't understand!' It is up to the teacher to repeat, smile, encourage and reinforce these coping strategies. It is also important to remember that intermediate and more advanced learners will need language phrases to enable them to react to situations, apologise, express feelings or explain a situation. Rather than saying, 'I'm sorry I'm late', they should be able to say, 'I'm sorry I'm late because the bus didn't come / my alarm clock didn't go off / I have had an argument with my mum!'

It is very difficult to take on a group of students from a colleague who has operated more or less in the TL and has used different rules to indicate when another language may be used. This is why it remains important to try to operate a departmental policy on what students need to know and use. If you find yourself in a situation where you want to achieve greater TL use with a reticent group, remember, it does *not* happen overnight. If *you* operate 100% in the TL, you risk total alienation.

---

### Teacher activity 3.6

If you are in an English language working environment, consider the extent to which your students know when and how to work in the TL and the non-TL. Can you help to make things clearer to them if you use the non-TL at times?

---

It is far better to set out small achievable goals – such as TL slots that gradually increase in time, or ten instructions to practise a week. Remember, you can do more with new learners than with ones who have acquired bad habits. If you are a newly qualified teacher, ask to observe colleagues and note how they encourage students to use the TL. Likewise, if you feel a bit stale, ask to see younger colleagues – we can all pick up at least a couple of useful tips concerning delivery by watching each other.

## Displays

Some international students may be thousands of miles from the TL country. Do try to bring the classroom alive with as many realia as possible. Signs and posters in the TL can easily be created. Equally appealing can be the students' own TL work or things downloaded from the Internet, such as daily news from a TL country. Older and younger learners can all be encouraged to draw/write/produce/research aspects of cultural or linguistic interest. This is especially important within a truly international context where whole-school policy seeks to emphasise the value of each student and their own cultural heritage. Ask your head teacher, principal or director for a prominent noticeboard outside the Languages area, and fill it with displays on themes from different year groups. Display also who is the linguist of the month. All these little things promote the causes of the FL department enormously, and indeed promote the use of the TL.

## Disruption

Colleagues report, and my own experience bears this out, that, when all else fails and teachers need to reprimand in the TL, the tone of voice, intonation and body language used all get the gist of the message across.

It is, however, well worth thinking about how excessive use of the TL, or inappropriate aims and expectations, may increase frustration in some students – especially low attainers. This may be totally different from your teaching context, but we all come across students who can behave in immature or unacceptable ways. They can be reprimanded in the TL. It is perhaps more constructive to think of keeping the pace of the lesson brisk – varying activities and how we use the TL, and varying what we expect from the students. If, at a general level, class discipline becomes problematic, it may be necessary to look closely at the level of difficulty of work set. Is it appropriate to the group? A variation of language presentation, seating positions and activities may be all that is needed. Make sure that different skills are practised so that you do not expect students to produce an hour of TL – it is unattainable and would be exhausting for both you and your students.

## Teaching students with a variety of mother tongues

Many of the issues already mentioned are equally applicable to students who do not have common mother or working tongues.

At the lower levels of language acquisition, problems can be avoided by making all new language situations as accessible as possible, for example by using a variety of visuals and introducing new language through more than one of the language skills. The challenge may arise when a point of structure needs to be explained. Strategies suggested by international colleagues have included asking the school librarian to find appropriate dual-language back-up resources in terms of grammar books and dictionaries, and finding in the school an older or more advanced learner of the same nationality or common working language to mentor the student. Such colleagues have often said, however, that many students are favoured in that they have very good language-acquisition skills across several languages – ones they have had to learn in order to survive in different linguistic and cultural contexts. It is refreshing that colleagues report this diversity in terms of its benefits rather than any potential disadvantages.

## Teaching and testing – the importance of the integration of the skills

The end point of teaching an FL is to enable our students to function independently in a TL setting that enables them to generate their own language and understand input outside the confines of narrow topic settings. The various skills of Listening, Speaking, Reading and Writing should not, therefore, be taught discretely. A well-planned lesson will generate opportunities for practice in different skills areas: oral work is also dependent upon Listening skills; Listening is likely to require Reading and Writing skills. The skills are interdependent and, if we are to devise an interesting and motivating approach to lessons, we need to adopt a coherent approach in class which aims to develop the various skills in an integrated way.

As Pachler and Field (2002: 103) state:

> progression does not take place within an isolated FL skill but across a number of skill areas. Therefore, successful FL lessons integrate a number of activities and exercises, developing different skills that are carefully chosen to build on previous knowledge and understanding.

Such an integration of skills and complementary skills development has long been accepted by both teachers in the classroom and authors of coursebooks. This approach has also been mirrored in terms of assessment. With the arrival of a communicative methodology, it was very apparent that tests of end-of-course measurement and achievement, such as CIE IGCSE, would have to reflect the tenets of communicative methodology whilst remaining reliable.

In testing terms, a good, robust test will strive to achieve high levels of both validity and reliability. Validity is the extent to which the test is successful in measuring what it purports to measure. Davies, A. (1968) saw one important type of validity (construct validity) as the extent to which a test reflects accurately the principles of a valid theory of FL testing. To have high validity, a test should reflect accurately the syllabus on which it is based (Woods 1993: 45), and it is to this effect that test designers and coursebook authors have defined the content of the examination syllabus in terms of topic areas, vocabulary and grammar structures.

There is, however, a danger in designing tests that reflect totally real-life situations and have high validity: they may lose some of their 'reliability'. Harrison (1983: 10) defines the reliability of a test as its consistency. Weir (1988: 34) states, 'The concern is with how far we can depend on the results that a test produces or, in other words, could the results be produced consistently?' A reliable test has to produce results consistently. This is crucial in terms of an examination such as CIE IGCSE, which tests large numbers of candidates and sets a standard that is recognised on a worldwide basis within the context of a variety of different educational systems.

The CIE IGCSE examinations were amongst some of the first FL achievement tests to attempt testing in the TL on a worldwide basis at this level of achievement. The four language skills were given an equal weighting (importance), but methods of examining Speaking/Listening skills meant that other skills such as Reading and/or Writing were also involved. Reading and Writing skills became integrated into one paper and a separate Writing (composition) paper was introduced to test accuracy of Writing. These examinations were designed and developed to show what candidates knew and could do; and this approach had to be reflected in the mark schemes, which stressed positive achievement. In the examination situation, candidates did not start with a notional 100% and lose marks. They started with zero marks and gained them. This reflected the methodological approach of communicative language teaching within the classroom. Elements of papers that tested Listening and Reading skills were marked for communication rather than accuracy of Writing.

For the first time, therefore, the underpinning test design really did attempt to have high validity whilst retaining reliability. Skills were integrated within test papers and testing was seen not just as a bolt-on, but as a complementary activity. This was important as testing can often influence the nature of what is taught and how it is taught. The 'backwash' of an examination, or the effect it has upon teaching, is now considered as an important element in testing, and it is highly desirable that testing of a summative nature (final examination of achievement) is seen to be complementary to the teaching and learning situation.

## Formative assessment

Chapters 4–7 will focus largely on summative testing. A summative test is a test that measures the sum total of what a student has learnt at the end of a course of study, for example CIE IGCSE or O Level.

A summative test is usually not set and marked by the class teacher, and is frequently administered by an external institution such as a ministry of education or awarding body such as CIE. Tests such as IGCSE and O Level are intended to be an end-of-course measure of learner achievement.

There exists, however, another type of assessment, which is classroom-based and which – when used properly – can have a crucial role to play in the teaching process. This is known as **formative assessment**. As teachers, we constantly make use of this type of assessment, but do we fully exploit its potential?

## Characteristics of formative assessment

One purpose of formative assessment is to enable teachers to use information gained about the learner's progress to inform and to help in the planning of future learning. In this sense, formative assessment can be seen to have a remedial aspect, in that a learner's progress is reviewed diagnostically and areas for improvement can be targeted.

Formative assessment is usually prepared and administered by a teacher on a regular basis and is linked directly to the teaching and learning that precede it. Traditionally, this will take the form of a discrete skill test or set of tests, usually topic-based, at the end of a unit or topic of work. However, a test can only really be termed formative if the teacher does not merely keep track of a learner's mark, but also acts upon this information and relates it to teaching and learning objectives. The focus of such testing is therefore on the process of learning rather than the result of learning.

I have worked in departments where formative assessment has been seen as termly tests involving the conversion of a raw mark to a percentage and then a ranking of the students. Students in such situations have seen tests in a very negative way, as a test of failure. It is therefore important, when considering the content of classroom tests, that clear and attainable learning objectives are made apparent to learners – and that the tests actually do test these learning objectives. The following are useful starting points to consider when designing tests for classroom use:

- To what extent are the students aware of what is being tested?
- Are students aware of how work is evaluated? Do they understand the system of marking?
- How useful is the feedback given by the teacher? Does it indicate errors, or does it indicate areas for further improvement?
- To what extent do students take responsibility for their part in the learning process? Do they keep track of their own progress and evaluate their own performance?
- At the end of the tests, is there an opportunity for students and teachers to evaluate future learning targets?

It is well worth addressing each of these points.

## Awareness of what is being tested

At the beginning of each unit of work it is desirable to set out the learning objectives for the group. These can, for example, be divided into communicative tasks (e.g. 'I can book a hotel room'), vocabulary tasks and linguistic structures / language tasks. Students keep their own list and can tick off the tasks as they progress. At the beginning of each lesson it is also desirable to write up on the board learning tasks for students, so that they can see where they are in their course of learning. Once they are aware of the programme of learning, they can be made far more aware of what is being tested. The above learning goals should be related to your schemes of work and it is helpful that most language coursebooks now give learning goals at the beginning of each unit of work.

## Raising students' awareness of how work is evaluated

Traditionally, FL teachers have used marking annotation based on a negative approach and error indication. As in the CIE IGCSE tests of Writing, a positive marking scheme can be used. If, for example, written work is being annotated, it is useful to explain that it may be marked for the messages communicated and also for its accuracy. It is of greater use in class tests to write a comment than to indicate and correct every error; students often take more notice of comments. Correction of errors by the teacher is frequently *not* acted on by learners. It can also be fruitful to underline areas of error and annotate the margin with a system such as *Vb* (verb), *T* (tense). This kind of annotation can be displayed in the classroom and given to students, enabling them to locate areas for improvement. It can actually help them to *think* about and rectify their mistakes.

## Pupil profiling and feedback

Students can be made more aware of their part in the learning process if they also keep track of their results. To this end it is useful to give each student a profile sheet. This can be a simple grid with the topic / learning stage indicated and space for ticks to be entered by the skills/tasks achieved. The ticks indicate where the students have been successful. Underneath, there is space for them to answer simple questions such as these:

- What have I enjoyed most in this unit?
- What have I found hard?
- What have I done well?
- What can I improve on?
- What are my learning targets?

If students attach their work to the profile sheet and keep it in an assessment folder, it is easy for them to keep track of their own progress. It is important at this final stage to devote a lesson to seeing the students, in order to set and agree attainable targets. Some students will need to be told to revisit certain areas of work as part of their targets, and may well need further support from the teacher. In my experience, however, they can often tell me what they need to do in order to make further progress. Indeed, several have asked me for a retest to prove to themselves that they have made progress.

If formative assessment is to be of real benefit, it must be viewed not simply as a type of test, but as part of a learning process which involves follow-up action. When used in this way, it will indeed be far more of a positive experience for the learner and, in my experience, will increase learner motivation.

## Teacher activity 3.7

Devise a simple student profile sheet that could be used for students in their final year of FL study for classroom-based tests.

## LOOKING BACK

- If you have been teaching for several years, consider the extent to which your own views on methodology may have evolved.
- To what extent does your approach reflect a communicative approach? What role do the teaching and learning of grammar play in your approach?
- What are the limitations placed upon the classroom and learners by the notion of authenticity?
- Do you consider the use of the TL important? If so, how can you maximise its use yourself and increase its use by learners?
- To what extent do you view the skills of Listening, Speaking, Reading and Writing as interdependent? Do your learning activities reflect this integration of skills?
- Does formative assessment feature in your learning programmes? If formative assessment does feature, how do you make use of the results? Are your students aware of the learning objectives and the outcomes?
- Are your students able to evaluate their own performance?
- Do the outcomes of assessment feed into future learning?

# 4 Teaching and assessing Listening skills

Chapters 1 to 3 have referred to the importance of an integrated skills approach within the classroom in terms of a learning and teaching context. This is mirrored in the way examinations such as the CIE IGCSE assess the various language skills. It is, however, crucial to consider the particular skills required for listening comprehension in order to facilitate sound lesson planning. To what extent are listeners passive or participatory, given that they need to respond to input?

Listening is a vital primary stage of language acquisition. If students do not listen or learn to listen well, then the latter stages of the complex pattern of language acquisition within a productive framework (in other words, Speaking and Writing) in the communicative classroom will simply not happen.

It is important to consider here the most significant elements that may block the Foreign Language (FL) learner's progress and how best the teacher may overcome such blocks. How best can we motivate our learners to listen confidently, and what are the best strategies to help them achieve sound Listening skills within our overall plan of attack?

## Learners' reactions within the Listening situation

My 20 years in the classroom, and observation of students during controlled Listening tests, have led to the following observations:

- Learners feel most threatened by a taped input when they have no control over the speed of input and no control over when to pause the delivery of this input. This can create high levels of anxiety, which blocks the ability to listen and respond effectively to input. As Hedge (2000: 255) states:

> the most vital element to listening is confidence that comes with practice and with achieving success from an early stage. The role of the teacher is to provide as much practice as possible by talking to learners . . . by exposing them to a range of materials in the classroom.

We often look on the listener as an eavesdropper but, as Hedge rightly points out, listening is often participatory and frequently features the integration of comprehension and speech.

- Listeners panic. They need to know exactly how many times a text will be repeated and where the pauses (if any) will be, so they know when to write their answers.
- Listeners tend to panic most about being lost in a fog of spoken foreign language. They need to have clear rubrics (examination instructions) and contextualisation, and to have tasks presented in the order of the text that is heard.
- Listeners need to be taught listening strategies such as predictive skills, and what to do whilst listening (see below).
- Post-Listening skills (i.e. integration with Reading/Writing skills) also need to be taught.
- In the test situation, students need to read carefully through rubrics and questions in order to be able to contextualise the material that is about to follow.
- If listeners have to respond in a written form, they worry that the accuracy or inaccuracy of their written response is an issue. In many examinations – such as the CIE IGCSE – inaccuracy of written Target Language (TL) is not an issue in the Listening paper, provided that the content/message of the response is clear. In such cases, candidates need to be reassured that the accuracy part of their Writing skills will be assessed only where relevant, for example in a Writing paper designed to test Writing skills.

## 'Bottom-up' and 'top-down' Listening skills

Nunan and Lamb (1995: 17) state a case for seeing good listeners as having 'bottom-up' and 'top-down' Listening skills. What are these skills?

- Bottom-up skills are analytical. Listeners demonstrating bottom-up skills 'segment the stream of speech into its constituent sounds, link these together to form words and chain the words together to form clauses and sentences'.
- Top-down skills involve the prior knowledge brought by the listener to the text. Such 'cultural' or 'world' knowledge helps the listener to understand a text and bring meaning to it. This knowledge, sometimes known as 'top-down' or 'world knowledge and contextualisation', is particularly relevant to international examinations. If questions are very culturally specific in context or specific to one geographic area of the globe, it is inappropriate to expect a global audience to bring the same top-down skills to the task.

- Consider a class you teach. Talk to them and ask them what they find most difficult when they listen to Listening material; for example, task (question), text (input), contextualisation, use of TL in the response to a text.
- Consider the speed of delivery of a text and the pauses. Do they make a difference?
- Consider the fact that one text could be used with a variety of response types (e.g. box ticking, short answers, multiple choice). Which response types do you consider to be the easiest and least stressful to students?

## To remember

As Nunan and Lamb (1995: 38) say: 'Listeners do both constructive and interpretative work in which they integrate what they know with what they know about the world.'

The next section of this chapter will examine how best to enhance our students' Listening skills in the teaching and testing situations.

## Improving Listening skills – how to acquire technique

Here are some important facts and recommendations to consider:

- Each time you or your students use the TL in class for transactional purposes, you are increasing Listening skills. Do not let opportunities escape!
- Your coursebook will probably include a variety of styles. Read the transcripts and listen to the tapes before lessons, and assess whether the style of textual input has any effect on your students' ability to cope with listening for key details and/or listening for general understanding (gist).
- Plan lessons so that at least one taped activity is used – this exposure will decrease the fear factor. Remember to go through the instructions such as times played, pauses and so on. Tell students how they will be assessed for comprehension.
- Choose a coursebook that has good taped material – ask for an inspection copy of the tape/CD. Speed of delivery is important. It should not be too fast.
- Ask students to read the questions in an exercise before attempting it. Ask them to predict the **content** of the passage to be heard. It is not crucial that this be done in the TL. This sort of exercise encourages them to practise their predictive skills, which will help them to cope with both the expected and the unexpected/unpredictable elements of a text/response.

- Encourage students to read the questions in an exercise and guess at **responses** before they hear a text. This helps them to assimilate language which may be needed in both the question and the text.
- Encourage students to identify the topic/context of a text. You may like to set homework that will introduce the vocabulary before they are confronted with the text.
- Refer to the examination syllabus and the defined content. Remember that, if students encounter any problems on the day, these should not be with the format (types of questions used) but with the form (textual input).
- Encourage students to be daring. Stop a tape in class and ask, 'What happens/happened next?' This encourages them to feel more confident about using linguistic skills.
- Tell students that the hallmark of a good learner is knowing they do *not* need to understand every word. Tell them that language learning is not an exact science and that good, 'informed' guessing is feasible as a method of answering. Point out that this may be a matter of deduction rather than guesswork. Intuitive guessing based on ruling out incorrect answers may be totally appropriate, and it is a valid way of arriving at a correct response.

## How can learners listen more effectively?

Richards (1990: 59–60) gives a list of what learners need to be able to do in order to listen effectively:

### Bottom-up processes

- retain input while it is being processed
- recognise word divisions
- recognise key words in utterances
- recognise key transitions in discourse
- use knowledge of word-order patterns to identify constituents in utterances
- recognise grammatical relations between key elements in sentences
- recognise the function of word stress in sentences
- recognise the function of intonation in sentences

### Top-down processes

- use key words to construct the schema of a discourse
- construct plans and schema from elements of a discourse
- infer the role of the participants in a situation
- infer the topic of a discourse
- infer the outcome of an event

- infer the cause or effect of an event
- infer unstated details of a situation
- infer the sequence of a series of events
- infer comparisons
- distinguish between literal and figurative meanings
- distinguish between facts and opinions

## Teacher activity 4.2

- Consider the kinds of Listening tasks you present to your students. Do they stress bottom-up or top-down Listening skills, or both kinds of skills?
- Consider a group of less able students – try to design a short Listening task linked to your present topic of study that would stress bottom-up skills.
- Consider a group of more able students. Try to design a short Listening task linked to your present topic of study which would go beyond bottom-up skills.
- Which do you think are the more 'sophisticated' – the harder – skills, from the students' point of view? Why are these skills more challenging?
- Refer to the Curriculum Content section of the CIE IGCSE syllabus for FL, Paper 1 – Listening. Which skills do you think are tested in the Core and Supplement?

# Linking the teaching and testing objectives
## Core Listening skills

The CIE IGCSE syllabus Curriculum Content for Listening states that Core students should be able to 'demonstrate understanding of specific detail in short, formal public announcements, informal announcements, short conversations and interviews' and 'demonstrate general comprehension of the above'.

Students are therefore expected to understand key vocabulary within short utterances and factual information within a variety of timeframes (tenses) – past, present and future. The textual input likely to be encountered is also stated in the syllabus, as follows:

### Section 1

a) Short recordings (one or two sentences), some involving two speakers, tested mainly by visual material.
b) Recordings containing factual information about travel, weather, opening times, facilities available.

## Section 2

Recordings containing information which will be of interest to the candidate without directly concerning him/her: conversations, discussions, simple radio programmes such as news, current affairs, interviews, factual reports are likely sources.

Within the testing context, it is crucial to consider difficulty, not just of task in terms of question type, but also in terms of textual input (e.g. speed, density and length of text). Test-setters work to a tight descriptive framework of both task and text type in order to ensure parity of difficulty from one year to the next. They also pay close attention to vocabulary and topic lists so as to ensure that demands placed on candidates remain fair. Setters use a variety of question types that require different types of response from candidates. This is very important as listeners are not passive (and most certainly not within a testing context, as they must listen and respond); they are participators. The forms of response required must be varied so as to enable candidates to have the best possible chance of showing what they have understood. Some of the question types frequently used are these:

### Objective
- multiple choice (visuals) (tick one of four);
- multiple choice (tick one or more) using verbal cues or visuals;
- ticking the true statements in a longer list of statements;
- filling gaps using one word from three options;
- grid filling (note completion of a short nature).

### Non-objective
- short answers to questions in the TL.

The wider the choice of question types, the more unlikely it is that candidates will be adversely affected by the format of a question type at which they may not excel. Weir and Roberts (1994) and others cite the need to have a good array of testing types.

All the above question types feature in modern coursebooks, and this serves to underline the need to choose a coursebook with good taped input covering a variety of textual input and question types.

Consider your coursebook. Is it offering students a variety of Listening inputs and task types? If not, do not panic – you may be able to purchase an additional set of Listening practice books.

## Extended Listening skills

More able students need to be pushed beyond the factual and the understanding of clearly stated opinions. The CIE IGCSE Curriculum Content states that, in addition to the Core skills outlined above, Extended students should be able to:

- demonstrate general and specific understanding of longer and more complex material
- identify the important points or themes of the material, including attitudes, emotions and ideas that are expressed
- draw conclusions from and identify relationships between ideas within the material.

In addition to showing analytical (bottom-up) skills, students will need to rely heavily on top-down skills. It is crucial also to consider the textual input. The CIE IGCSE syllabus in FL describes Paper 1, Section 3, recordings as:

Recordings of discussions between 2 or 3 people on a subject of mutual interest: holiday plans, recalling a shared experience, etc. Questions will test appreciation of the speakers use of language to express agreement or disagreement, apologies or complaints, attitudes, emotions and ideas, etc as well as understanding of the gist of their conversation.

So, this involves a move away from the factual and straightforward towards the language of comparison and inference. Students may need to assess in terms of preferences, or contrast one set of opinions with those heard from another speaker. The textual input is longer and students need to be able to process information whilst responding. Pauses and reading time are given, but it is well worth pointing out to students that answers in the TL should be kept short and to the point – they should aim to get the message across.

## Increasing students' participation in Listening activities

The biggest challenge, as seen above, is how to increase students' confidence. Listening can be seen to be a passive activity (as in eavesdropping on a conversation), but we need to increase our students' ability to participate in the listening process if we are to motivate them and increase their confidence levels.

As well as accustoming our students to a range of different textual inputs, it is important to practise with them a range of different activities. These can vary from simple body language (e.g. putting up a hand in response to a true/false check), to responding via writing (e.g. grids, answering written questions and ticking boxes). Students can be asked to respond as a group or as individuals. It is even more fruitful if some kind of game element can be introduced into the process.

Most teachers tend to feature Listening coursebook material as part of their presentation of new language, and this is most usually exploited via objective questions (ticking boxes, grids, etc.). There are, however, other sources of input that should not be dismissed and which can be exploited in a variety of ways.

## The teacher as a resource

You are the best model (and probably the least threatening, as you can aid comprehension via talking with gestures and using visuals). Prepare a short text linked to your topic content (e.g. holidays) and, either on the board or on the OHP, prepare a grid with key words such as *Where?*, *When?*, *With whom?*, *Activities?*, *Length of stay?*, *Likes?*, *Dislikes?* Students should be told that you will repeat your text two or three times, and that you may split up your text and pause wherever you feel this to be appropriate. It is of course necessary to check that students are familiar with key vocabulary items, and this activity works best as a starter to a new lesson which is recycling the previous lesson's language, or as a mid-lesson activity in which the first stage has been the presentation of new vocabulary / key phrases. The student should ideally be giving short responses – single words or short phrases in the TL. Do remind them that incorrect spelling is not an issue (unless you wish it to be), as you are checking that the message has been understood. Once the activity is completed, it is important to review things together. At this stage it is very useful for students to see a written version of what has been heard, so that a link is established between the skills and in order for the written word to support what has been heard. Encourage students to keep a record of their marks for Listening, and give them a mark for which they should be aiming. Also ask them to try to identify vocabulary problem areas or structures which posed a problem.

## The student as a resource

The above activity can be exploited further when students are a little more confident about the topic area and feel able to write simple accounts of their own holidays. These can be in the form of monologues or interviews. Other students can be asked either to note down details (as above) or to tick multiple-choice responses provided by the teacher. It is important when asking students to produce such accounts that they are given a plan in advance which features the categories of information required. More able learners could be asked as a final stage to say which person seemed to like/dislike their holiday most and why. This exercise works well; students like to listen to each other and, given that you can monitor the early stages of their accounts, you can have some control over the vocabulary and structures used. With more able learners, accounts can be more spontaneous and student response could become freer (e.g. note-taking).

## Video/CD room as a resource

If you are fortunate enough to have access to a video and computers, a huge variety of Listening resources is now available. (Chapter 8 deals with some of these resources and gives ideas for exploiting them.) Videos that are produced to accompany courses can be very useful. They enable students to put language into context, and visual clues aid understanding. As with any input, however, careful preparation of the best kind of participatory activity is required. If the aim is listening/watching for pleasure, you may not want to ask students to write responses, but it is still helpful to listeners to preview the context of the language and structures/vocabulary likely to be heard. Oral feedback to check understanding is desirable. When I use video clips myself, I always prepare a simple quiz sheet for students to fill in after a preliminary viewing. It increases motivation and makes viewers watch/listen with a purpose. Students may have a tendency to view lazily unless we devise meaningful tasks. A good follow-up stage to a quiz activity is to ask students to go on to write simple dialogues similar to ones they have viewed. If you have a video camera in school, the dialogues can be taped and viewed by the group. In the past, my groups have produced a guide to their school on videotape, a fashion show, holiday programmes and a guide to their home town for visitors.

## Cassettes as a resource

If students have access to a Walkman, then a whole host of activities is possible. Firstly, you can ask them to copy coursebook materials onto an individual cassette. These can be exploited for individual study / homework activities. This is admittedly time consuming to organise with a large group, but well worth the effort. It enables students to stop and start tapes where they want and lessens the fear factor, as they are at least in charge of how much they hear at once.

If you can arrange a class link with a school in a TL country, you can ask students to prepare short spoken accounts about themselves, their region and so on, and send a collective cassette abroad. In return you may receive a wonderful variety of authentic material on cassette which you can exploit in class. The direct contact with a group of young people in the TL country is highly motivating and may have a rewarding spin off into Speaking, Reading and Writing skills. Students really enjoy participating in such a group project, and the initial stages of preparing individual spoken accounts may lead into other possibilities – such as group Listening, drafting and redrafting of written work, and helping each other. These are all interpersonal communicative skills to be valued highly in the FL classroom.

## Older students as a resource

If you have an FL assistant, then it goes without saying that they are a valuable resource. One source of input, however, which is frequently forgotten is the older / more advanced learner. I make use of older learners by asking them in to talk in the FL to younger groups about the topic being studied. They can read accounts or perform dialogues. It is well worth making older learners language monitors/prefects. They can be used in the ways mentioned above as well, and provide yet more variety in the TL classroom.

### Teacher activity 4.4

- Prepare an initial Listening text which exploits you as a resource. Base this on a topic you are teaching to a group of senior students, and then prepare a matching worksheet using headings which will require your students to respond via short responses in the form of a grid.
- Using the above sheets, develop the idea further so that students can be used as resources. Could the same grid be used?
- Think of different ways to encourage students to participate and be less passive in the Listening situation. Think of their types of response to stimulus material and try to include at least three types of response in your next lesson plan.

Here is a checklist of participatory activities in response to Listening input:
- Students raise hands in response to true/false questioning.
- Students respond in oral or written form.
- Students play games such as Bingo/Lotto which require circling/ticking of correct answers.

- Students draw a response (e.g. a person in a unit of work based on personal descriptions).
- Students hear half an account and say/write what will come next (good for able learners).
- Students listen to songs whilst looking at an incomplete transcript. They have to work out the missing words (a list of missing words may or may not be supplied). Ask them to complete the activity against a stopwatch in order to include a game element.
- Students choose words missing from a script from pairs of words which feature different spellings/sounds. (This is a good activity for encouraging bottom-up skills.)
- Students tick and number visuals according to the order in which they hear things on a tape.
- Students match short statements (true/false) to what they hear. They can use either the language heard on tape or (for more advanced learners) similair phrases and synonyms.
- Students mime actions to a story you read out (good for younger learners, who enjoy games such as Simon Says).
- Students match a short written account to what they hear on tape and say how it differs. (This is a more demanding activity, which will require you to prepare a worksheet at variance with an account/dialogue taken, for example, from a coursebook. It works well, for instance, with extracts featuring people buying things in different shops and at different prices.)
- Students 'phone' each other in class; the rest of the group act as message-takers (e.g. arranging outings, dates, times) and note down details.
- Students listen to a short news broadcast and weather report. You place a list of headings on the board. They have to match up the order of the items heard. (More detail can be required of more advanced learners.)

This is by no means an exhaustive list, but it is given to stimulate your ideas. All of the above have been used by international teachers, and I am indebted to them for their suggestions. Finally, if you do not have access to a huge taped library of resources, do not despair – remember that every time you practise Speaking skills, you are increasing Listening skills. It is crucial to have a coursebook that has good taped material, but with a little ingenuity we can ourselves provide good additional materials and make our students more confident and involved in the listening process.

## LOOKING BACK

◆ How useful is it to have an understanding of top-down and bottom-up approaches to Listening skills?
◆ How do you encourage such approaches in your own learners?
◆ What have you learned about the importance of a gradient of difficulty in Listening exercises?
◆ Which kinds of Listening exercises feature in your lesson plans?
◆ Which features do you feel to be important when designing Listening exercises?
◆ To what extent do your learners participate in Listening activities?

# 5 Teaching and assessing Speaking skills

## Introduction

The developments in teaching methodology in the 1980s and 1990s have led to much more emphasis being placed on our students' ability to speak and communicate effectively in the Target Language (TL). Recent teaching materials reflect this approach, as do Speaking tests such as the CIE IGCSE Speaking Test.

As discussed in Chapter 2, one cannot stress enough the interdependence of the four skills. Speaking effectively depends very much on the speaker's ability to interact with an interlocutor. Successful Speaking cannot therefore take place without effective Listening skills. Speakers must pay attention to their listeners, and adapt their own responses and questions according to the needs of the listeners. As teachers, therefore, we need to set up learning activities which enable students to interact both with ourselves as models of the TL (see Chapter 1) and with each other. Such activities will be discussed below.

One current model of language teaching, 'presentation – practice – communication' (Cajkler and Addelman 2000: 33), emphasises the importance of the teacher's oral input and the learner's practice and repetition of the oral model in the acquisition of the TL. We cannot expect learners to produce the spoken word without a significant input. For many teachers, such input in an initial phase of a lesson will be based on oral and aural activities, which in turn lead to a practice phase based on Speaking and Listening activities. In Chapter 3 the crucial role of the teacher's own use of the TL was discussed. Students cannot be expected to perform in the TL without a positive and reinforcing framework, and this chapter should be read in conjunction with earlier observations concerning the amount of TL use within the classroom.

Testing Speaking skills is frequently the area that worries teachers (whether new or experienced) most in that they themselves know that their own performance can hinder or help students in the examination room. They worry primarily about their own role and how to elicit the best from their students. Another area of concern is exemplified in a question often heard in teacher-training sessions: 'How can I be sure I am marking fairly?' Speaking tests require organisation so that you can concentrate on the students and their performance whilst retaining your sanity. Oral testing is demanding, but there is nothing quite as satisfying at the end of a teaching course and the completion of Speaking tests as the realisation that each student has had about 15 minutes of undivided attention (a rare thing in many schools), and that they have had the opportunity to show that they *can* communicate in a foreign language.

A Speaking test can only test the skills acquired over an examination course if these skills have been practised on a regular basis in the classroom. In some international classrooms this may present no problems as there may only be a few students with a similar level of foreign language skills, but in others there may be over 30 students, some of whom have very different levels of ability. Setting up and devising interesting activities may therefore be more of a challenge to the teacher. There is also the issue that in some classrooms Reading and Writing may be judged by students themselves to be 'real work', whereas Speaking 'does not matter as much'! Different countries and different teachers may have different approaches to the integration of Speaking skills in a teaching/learning programme, but it remains important to encourage and train students from Day 1 to communicate orally, with both the teacher and other students.

This chapter will consider the acquisition and practice of Speaking skills and suggest activities to encourage and motivate learners. It will also consider how best to carry out and assess Speaking tests so that both you and your students feel more confident about a formal end-of-course Speaking examination, such as the CIE IGCSE Speaking Test.

## Understanding Speaking objectives

What are our goals in terms of Speaking skills for our learners? From the assessment perspective, the CIE IGCSE syllabus for Foreign Languages (FL) defines the one global assessment objective as 'Communication'. Speaking is one of the four subskills incorporated in this one objective. The basic premise is that the spoken language is language used with a purpose. The CIE IGCSE syllabus states that its aims are to enable students to 'develop the ability to use the language effectively for purposes of practical communication within the country of residence, where appropriate, and in all countries where the language is spoken'.

## How does this translate into effective teaching goals?

Most teachers would agree that we are trying to instil into our learners the ability to move from a closely structured and guided use of language (such as repetition) to the generation of freer and much less guided language of a personalised nature which satisfies a perceived communicative need. Pachler and Field (2002) cite this as a progression from repetition to structured pairwork to open-ended role play. One helpful definition I use in CIE IGCSE training sessions is the move from dependence to independence – to what extent can the speaker cope unaided in a given TL context?

In teaching terms, this means that individual lessons and units of work need to afford a variety of tasks which reflect a hierarchy of difficulty and diminishing support from the teacher in terms of activities. Cajkler and Addelman (2000: 40) cite this notion of 'diminishing support' and give examples of Speaking activities (below) which one could use with 14–16-year-olds, based on a presentation – practice – communication model:

- Presentation: For less able students, the teacher mimes the actions and presents vocabulary and phrases, for example *il danse* (he dances), *il tricote* (he knits), *il nage* (he swims) or past-time equivalents, depending on the stage of learning.
- Practice:
  – Repetition of phrases and vocabulary
  – Responding to flashcards
  – Responding to teacher questions (all abilities, as the questions can be graded to suit learners' abilities and interests)
  – Pairwork with cue cards
  – Survey/questionnaire on hobbies (can cater for a range of abilities)
- Communication: Talking freely about one's leisure, for example, to the foreign language assistant, to peers, visitors.

Cajkler and Addelman (2000) refer to the early stages of Speaking as skill-getting pre-communicative activities and the later stages as skill-using communicative activities. The more advanced the learner becomes, the more risks they are willing to take, and this will necessitate sympathetic monitoring and error correction from the teacher. Overcorrection of spoken language can induce anxiety in learners and can discourage students from wanting to generate their own language. It is perhaps better to correct during the more controlled stage in a supportive and encouraging way, and then allow speakers to make errors and move on – correcting in a later group exercise when individuals have had the chance to experiment and actually make errors. The notion of freeing up our learners must go hand-in-hand with the idea that errors will be made, and individual teachers need to develop their own consistent approach to how best to correct errors and reinforce correct models in their given situation.

When moving from the guided to the freer stage of Speaking skills, the dynamics of the learning situation change. Initially, at a presentation stage, learners will frequently be in a whole-class situation, and will later move on – perhaps to pair/group work – before finally ending up as a whole class again. Ideally, this should free up the teacher to move around and monitor before drawing the class back together to recap, correct and reinforce the language points and aims of the lesson.

## Teacher activity 5.1

- Consider the ways in which you present new work. Do you think you give adequate practice time before you ask students to move on to different language skills activities (e.g. Reading/Writing)?
- Consider your own Speaking activities. Do you think it important to include Speaking activities in each lesson?
- Think of a typical lesson for 14–15-year-old learners. Think of two pre-communicative and two communicative Speaking activities.

## Organisational implications for the teacher

In order to open up a variety of tasks and activities, the management of the classroom is vital. It is a sad, but true, fact that colleagues in other departments have often commented upon the noise emanating from the corridors of FL departments. I reply that this is controlled and 'busy' noise, not wild chaos! To ensure that speakers remain on task during pairwork, there are several crucial points to observe:

- Speakers *must* be given a clear task with an achievable and purposeful outcome.
- All must feel involved and have the opportunity to practise what has been presented.
- Correction is carried out in a non-threatening way.
- A clear model of what is to be done is given to students before they are expected to perform.
- The teacher should set a time limit for completion of the task, and should monitor problems the students may be encountering.
- The teacher has a clearly defined signal, such as clapping their hands, which should immediately be recognised by students as a sign that a return from pair or group work to the class situation is now required. If this is not firmly in place, anarchy can break out. Pairwork can work only if a rule is set up on Day 1 that, if the teacher is talking, the class should return to 'class listening'.

Points to observe in whole-class Speaking activities when they are teacher led are:

- Use a variety of presentation techniques. Visuals help enormously in the stage of acquisition and give memory 'hooks' to learners. An OHP is invaluable.
- Repeat key words/phrases several times, and use a variety of repetition techniques using individuals, boys/girls, half the class, whole class.
- Encourage students to mime activities in response to your speech.
- Ask a variety of questions which require different forms of response. For example, 'I'm cooking, yes or no?' (response 'Yes' or 'No'); 'Am I cooking or writing?' (response 'Writing').
- Ask open-ended questions such as 'What are you doing?' (plus flashcard as stimulus) at the end of your sequence of questions. Remember to diminish your support gradually.
- Give the student a flashcard and make them 'own' the associated word/phrase. This can lead to some excellent questioning from other students. For example, 'Have you got the swimming pool?' (student has the castle). Student responds, 'No, I've not got the swimming pool.' The student who gets the reply 'yes' gets the flashcard.
- Try to introduce a challenge/game element to increase motivation. (Some ideas feature in the next section.)
- Spread your questions around the class.
- Try to keep your use of TL at a maximum level, with all instructions in the TL (see Chapter 3 for suggestions about how to achieve this).
- Remember to praise and smile – to keep motivation levels high.

## Teacher activity 5.2

- Consider how you organise Speaking work in your classroom. Do you concentrate on teacher-led whole-class situations, or do you give pairwork opportunities?
- Consider management implications – do you have a clear strategy / set of rules which operates when students are working together? If not, devise a checklist to give to students.
- Consider your presentation techniques. Do you use visuals? Ask groups of younger learners to help you devise classroom displays of new work (e.g. leisure activities, food, house/home). Use the best ones as a new set of flashcards and display the others in the room so that you can move round and point to different visuals.

# A checklist of Speaking activities
## Role play
Ur (1981: 9) states that for role play:

> the class is usually divided into small groups — often pairs — which are given situations and roles to act out and explore. This acting is done for the sake of the language and imaginative activity, not for exhibition; though some students may occasionally enjoy seeing or showing off some particularly successful scene. The various groups, therefore, are activated simultaneously.

Role play can be closely guided, with a predefined script on a board or OHP which may require students to change just a few words or numbers. Such scripts will feature newly presented words/phrases such as buying tickets or visiting a café. Role play can also be freer or more open; for example, participants at a more advanced level could be asked to act out ringing a friend to make arrangements to go out. The advantage of such activities is that the purpose is very clear to students and the teacher can control how much (or little) support to give them.

## Presentation
Students are asked to make a presentation on a topic of a certain duration (to be decided by the teacher). This is a very good end-of-topic activity. Students can perform their topics on tape, in small groups or, if trust levels are high and classroom confidence good, in front of the whole class. Even young learners can often speak for up to a minute on a topic and, as learners grow more confident, they really enjoy hearing themselves and take considerable pride in being able to sustain speech in the FL. Cue cards can be used in class to aid memory. There is an added game element if groups use stopwatches against each other.

## General conversation/discussion
The face-to-face conversation remains one of the best ways to engage speakers. It builds upon the question–answer work that is the very essence of the FL classroom. In face-to-face encounters, speakers learn to adjust responses to the needs of their interlocutor. They personalise language, and can show their ability to move from coping with simple, predictable questions to more open, unpredictable ones that require a freer and more open response. More sophisticated users of language can also show their ability to use a variety of tenses or timeframes. (A fuller treatment of how best to elicit good performances in the conversation situation can be found later in this chapter, in the assessment section.)

## Information-gap activities

These activities could be said to be an extension of role-play activities. Scrivener (1994: 62) describes the aim of such activities as 'to get students to use the language they are learning to interact in realistic and meaningful ways, usually involving exchanges of information'. The activity depends on one person possessing information which the other one does not have. The task can only be completed if the pair work together (e.g. partner A needs to complete a journey and B has the timetable). Simple cue cards with tasks can be made to support such activities, and students can be asked to record in written form the answers to the tasks on the cards. This in turn can lead to the practice of other skills (Reading, Writing). Typical information-gap activities which work at an IGCSE level are situations such as negotiating dates for a trip (partner A has one set of dates/problems on a card, B has a different set of dates/opportunities) or trying to make a reservation at a hotel (partner A) when B (the receptionist) may have only certain dates available (length of stay, facilities needed and price can be negotiated).

## Group discussion

Given the level of achievement of the typical IGCSE learner, group discussion will often be beyond all but the most advanced learner; it requires a level of language which goes beyond the factual, and it relies very much on not only the giving of opinions but also explanation, justification and inference. Successful group discussion depends on many factors. Examples are equal participation in a group, the character of the individuals, and their desire to stand up to the opinions of others and participate within a group setting. For a group discussion to work, it is necessary for the teacher to define a clear task and to equip students with the language they will need to state opinions. It is of little use to say, for instance, 'Talk about holidays together.' An alternative scenario should instead be devised, in which a group has to decide where they will go on holiday together (aim) and each character is given a clear role which includes likes/dislikes and the money they have available. Careful preparation in linguistic terms should be given to constructions such as these:

- I'd prefer to go to . . . because . . .
- I don't like . . . because it's too expensive/far/noisy/boring.
- That's an awful idea. Let's go to . . . instead.

Ideally, students should have a preparation phase in which they can formulate ideas and take notes. Once they start on the task, the role of the teacher is to monitor but to keep a back seat. Over-involvement can stifle the desire of the group members to participate freely. If the teacher imposes a time limit, the activity will be more focused. At the end of the exercise, group feedback is invaluable in terms of both the communicative outcome and the linguistic needs of the group.

## Further suggestions for Speaking activities

Different teachers have different ways of presenting and practising new vocabulary and structures. Some use flashcards, some use tapes, some use OHPs and some a variety of approaches (including themselves as a model). The following suggestions are by no means exhaustive or prescriptive, but they are all activities that have worked well in class and could be adapted to suit learners of different ages and levels in the FL classroom.

- **Banks of questions.** These can be built into booklets with (or without) answers, useful for pairwork and preparation of presentations. Students can tape themselves or do oral homework if they have a tape-recording facility themselves or have access to one at school. (This takes no longer to mark than a set of exercise books.)
- **Role-play cards.** Students can work from very structured models presented on the board or OHP, with highlighted words that they need to replace (e.g. hotel requirements or train requirements). A variation on this is to remove some of the support and ask the student to provide more of the text. A final stage is to give the student cards written in either their own language or the TL (see past examination papers for models for older students), or using visuals. Students start initially in a class group but gradually move towards pairwork. Alternatively, as a final activity, students write their own situations. Younger learners especially may like to act them out.
- **Dice games.** Keep a set of dice. Six questions based on any topic being studied can be put on the board/OHP. Students have to shake the dice and answer the question that corresponds to the number on the dice. It is possible to put pictures on larger dice (e.g. of leisure activities); these can be used to cue what you did last weekend / will do next weekend, allowing for revision of tenses.
- **Memory games.** Examples include 'I went to the market and bought . . . ' (each student repeats the last article bought and adds a fresh one). Try to get the group to do this at speed and improve on their last performance. This works well with younger learners. Another example is based on putting 10–12 pictures on the OHP – each is numbered. Students practise the language for each picture together. The pictures are then gradually removed and the teacher asks what is missing. The aim is to get them to remember all 12, either in groups or as a class activity. This can be used for vocabulary groups or things such as holiday/leisure activities for which longer structures are needed.

- **The tray game.** First-year learners love this one. Up to 15 items are placed on a tray (or OHP transparency). Students have one minute to look and then one minute to recount them to a partner, who makes a list and reads it back to the class.
- **The hat game.** Topic titles (e.g. *My family*, *My hobbies*) are put in a hat or box. Students pull one out and have to speak for as long as possible or a certain time. (This works well as a revision task for 14–16-year-olds). It is a useful and productive lesson filler for the odd five minutes before the bell. (My own students like to mark each other.)
- **Students visit a website.** They research (or read a tourist brochure about) an interesting capital city, with the aim of spending a certain amount of time and money. They have to give an oral summary of what they did / would like to do. This works well with older learners (14–16-year-olds).
- **Students look at three or four pictures in a picture story.** They then have to predict what will happen next, or did happen.
- **If I were a . . .** This is a game which can be used at any level. It's very useful for practising animals, food, sports, leisure objects and so on. Young learners could say, 'If I were a toy, I'd like to be a teddy bear / a Gameboy' and so on. More able students can add a reason why. Still more sophisticated learners could do 'If I were a country' or 'If I were a famous person'. They can be encouraged to add linguistic structures and reasons/explanations.
- **Students script and record a guided tour to their school/town.** This could be a very rewarding final outcome based on a topic approach at the end of teaching.
- **The balloon game.** Able students like this, but it requires preparation. Each student picks a famous person and pretends to be that person. They have to say what good things they have achieved and why they deserve a place in a hot air balloon – which is descending rapidly! The loser gets thrown out. This works well with able learners.

Many of the above ideas require teacher preparation, cards, pictures and so on. But, once made, these resources last. If stored in the department, they can provide good language practice again and again. Also, if you have a large teaching group, such activities can be useful for making the students *talk to each other*, rather than the whole emphasis when speaking being placed on the teacher–student interaction. More importantly, they can be fun and may motivate some FL students. If students see Speaking activities as the norm from the first day in the FL classroom, and are used to TL classroom commands and requests, activities such as the above will be easier to operate. It may well be worth while to look at departmental teaching programmes and re-evaluate schemes of work in terms of what students are expected to achieve in spoken language by the end of each unit of work. In a classroom where teaching is frequently in the TL and a clear programme of commands / requests / game rules has been worked on from early days, setting up such activities is obviously easier.

There are many games which can be incorporated into the classroom, and the above are just a few ideas which many international teachers have used successfully.

## Assessing Speaking skills

This part of the chapter is intended to give a clear outline of what is required of both the teacher and the candidate in a formal end-of-course Speaking test such as the CIE IGCSE Speaking Test. Different elements of the test content are described, and advice is offered on how to apply the positive marking scheme. Finally, advice on how to get the best from candidates is given, along with practical guidance on how to set up and conduct the tests.

### Understanding Speaking assessment objectives

The CIE IGCSE syllabus for FL defines the one assessment objective as 'Communication', and Speaking is one of the four subskills incorporated in this. All candidates take a Speaking test, which has an equal weighting to the other skills.

So, what is being tested and how? The underpinning feature of the test is assessing *language used with a purpose.* The whole framework depends on the positive emphasis of testing what the candidate *is able to communicate* in a foreign language rather than what they cannot do. The fundamental principle when assessing is rewarding what is right, and not penalising what is wrong.

The 15-minute test gives candidates of all abilities the chance to show how well they can perform on a variety of tasks. Face-to-face interviews of this kind are reliable indicators of oral ability.

### Elements of the Speaking test

i    2 role play situations of 5 tasks each = 30 marks

ii    Topic conversation = 30 marks

iii    General conversation = 30 marks

(Impression: at the end of the test an Impression mark is awarded out of 10 marks)

Total marks = 100

## Role plays

The two role plays are targeted at different levels of candidate ability. Role play A aims to test factual transactions such as times, simple requests and questions, and requires candidates both to take the initiative and to respond. The topics and tasks of this role play come from Areas A, B and C of the Defined Content of the CIE IGCSE syllabus in FL. Role play B is designed not only to assess the above, but also to test tasks that might require notions such as apologising or persuading to be conveyed. This may necessitate the use of different tenses or more sophisticated structures in order to achieve communication in an accurate and appropriate way. The mark schemes (see below) feature the criteria of both communication and linguistic accuracy.

## Presentation / Topic conversation

Candidates are required to choose a topic prior to the test, and make an initial presentation on this subject for one to two minutes (maximum). The remaining three or four minutes of this section of the test are spent in discussion of the topic. The syllabus states that candidates should be able to 'report, express opinions and respond to questions on a topic of the candidate's choice'.

In the role-play section of the Speaking test, examiners evaluate candidates' performance on the basis of their ability to complete a series of prescribed tasks, which the candidate may (or may not) be able to do. The difficulty levels are set by CIE. In the presentation / topic conversation section the task is open and the examiner therefore has to evaluate candidate performance in terms of 'outcome'. The mark scheme for the topic conversation makes use of ascending mark bands which feature specific descriptions of levels of performance. The descriptions are based on both comprehension/responsiveness (the communicative features) and linguistic content (accuracy and use of structures).

Different levels of performance can (and should) be elicited from candidates of different abilities by examiners asking different kinds of questions. These questions obviously need to be aimed at the appropriate level for individual candidates. Some candidates will be able to understand basic factual questions only and will give such information back using simple subject–verb accords only. Others may be able to go beyond the factual, giving and explaining opinions and answering open questions beginning 'Tell me about . . . '. In linguistic terms, candidates are rewarded for their ability to use a range of tense and structures. If candidates have not used a range of tenses in the presentation of the topic, it is of paramount importance for the examiner to ask questions to enable them to display their knowledge of different tenses in the follow-up discussion on the topic.

## General conversation

The general conversation assessment objectives are very similar to those of the topic conversation and, indeed, the same marking bands are used. This final section (approximately five minutes) follows on from the topic conversation. The examiner is free to develop any point of interest, and can cover any number of topics according to the candidate's ability. As in the topic conversation, the candidate's performance is gauged by their responses to questions that elicit factual information (e.g. 'Where do you go to school?', 'What are you studying?'); and also, at the upper end of the range, by their responses to questions such as 'What would you change in your school?', 'Why?', 'What do you like most/least here?', 'Tell me about your future plans.'

The candidate's response is assessed in terms of communication/responsiveness – how much has been understood by the candidate and to what extent the candidate's answer can be understood (15 marks). The linguistic quality of the response is assessed, again out of 15.

Generally, most examiners cover at least two or three topics of conversation in the five minutes allotted in this section. Subjects such as everyday life, ambitions, house/home, family, school, home town/country, free time, holidays and future plans are all suitable topics. The difference between the topic conversation and the general conversation is that the latter test is one of *unprepared* conversation. The candidate should not know in advance which topics will be covered on the day. Conversation on the various topic areas can and should be practised in the classroom, but there must be no pre-learnt sequences of questions and answers in the examination. Candidates should have sufficient command of the idiom, vocabulary and language to answer such questions as the examiner asks on the day. The underlying principle is to extend candidates as far as possible in a sympathetic way, so that they can work up through the mark bands according to their ability.

## Using a positive mark scheme – how do we assess?

Teachers new to marking the CIE IGCSE Speaking test often express their worries about 'getting the marking right'. It is usually the candidate's teacher who conducts and marks the tests, and experience would suggest that the teacher is by far the best person to do so. It is the teacher who knows the students best and knows how far they can be extended. The marking, however, may be new in that teachers may not be used to a scheme that works from the bottom of the scale upwards and on a *positive* basis. The tradition of working on a negative basis and knocking marks off an often unattainable 100% may be more familiar.

The most important thing for all markers to remember is that *consistency* of marking is crucial. A sample of tests is checked by CIE moderators, who then increase, decrease or make no change to marks in order to bring centres into line with the agreed standard. This method relies on the consistency of marking in a centre.

Almost as important is to have a trial run in which the teacher goes through a practice examination. This enables the teacher/examiner to experience the process of marking whilst examining. This *really* does get easier with practice. Marks awarded on the spot are usually the right ones. It is crucial to be able to mark on the spot – but this does mean that teachers/examiners must be very familiar with the mark scheme. If teachers are not, then they may fail to ask questions which will elicit the sort of answers that allow candidates to be placed in the mid- to higher-mark bands.

## Marking the role plays

There are five set tasks per role play (some of which may contain two elements, e.g. meeting place and time), with a possible three marks per task. Marks are awarded as follows:

| | |
|---|---|
| An accurate utterance which not only conveys the meaning but which is expressed in native idiom and appropriate register. Minor errors (adjective endings, use of prepositions, etc.) are tolerated. The utterance is intelligible and the task of communication is achieved. | 3 |
| The language used is not necessarily the most appropriate to the situation and may contain inaccuracies which do not obscure the meaning. | 2 |
| Communication of some meaning is achieved, but the native speaker would find the message ambiguous or incomplete. | 1 |
| The utterance is unintelligible to the native speaker. | 0 |

The examiner plays the part of a patient and well-disposed speaker with no knowledge of the candidate's first language. Candidates are required to give natural responses, not necessarily in the form of sentences. Short answers, if appropriate to the task, could be awarded 3 marks.

When marking, do not listen for mistakes, but work from the bottom of the scale upwards and think, 'What has the candidate achieved?'
- If there is nothing intelligible, award 0.
- If part of the task is achieved, or one of the two set elements is achieved, award 1. (Examiners may prompt and/or rephrase, but in so

doing should not give away vital vocabulary or provide the answer themselves. They should instead try to help the candidate by paraphrasing or querying pronunciation. The candidate may be able to work up to a mark of 2.)

- If the meaning of the task is clearly communicated but the language is inaccurate or inappropriate (e.g. wrong register, a familiar form of address used in a formal situation, or an incorrect subject–verb accord), award 2.
- If the task is communicated clearly and in accurate and appropriate language (minor errors, e.g. of preposition, are tolerated), award 3.

Teachers frequently ask what is a major error of accuracy. If a subject–verb accord or tense is incorrect, meaning may still be clear, so you may be able to award a mark of 2. For example:

EXAMINER
What time will you arrive at the hotel?

CANDIDATE
At 3 o'clock.
(3 marks—the answer is clearly communicated and, although brief, it is appropriate in context.)

CANDIDATE
I arriving at 3 o'clock.
(2 marks—the answer is clearly understandable, but the language is incorrect.)

CANDIDATE
I'll arrive / I will arrive / I'm going to arrive at 3 o'clock.
(A clear 3 marks.)

Briefly then, incomplete message = 1, complete message = 2, complete message well expressed = 3. Remember, you must know your role well and be clear about the set tasks to apply the scheme fairly. If you miss a task out, don't worry; go back to it and make a brief note on the mark sheet to indicate to the moderator what has happened. Also, remember that there are no half-marks. Decide on a mark and be consistent.

## Marking the topic conversation and general conversation

The following table shows how the marks are awarded for both the topic conversation and the general conversation (30 marks for each test).

Scale (a) marks refer to *what* is said (comprehension/responsiveness). Scale (b) marks refer to *how* it is said. Each candidate receives a mark under each of the two scales for both the topic and general conversation sections.

| Category | | Mark |
|---|---|---|
| Outstanding | (a) Not necessarily of native speaker standard. <br> (b) The highest level to be expected of the best IGCSE candidates. | 14–15 |
| Very good | (a) Generally understands questions first time, but may require occasional rephrasing. Can respond satisfactorily to both straightforward and unexpected questions. <br> (b) Wide range of mostly accurate structures, vocabulary and idiom. | 12–13 |
| Good | (a) Has no difficulty with straightforward questions and responds fairly well to unexpected ones, particularly when they are rephrased. <br> (b) Good range of generally accurate structures, varied vocabulary. | 10–11 |
| Satisfactory | (a) Understands straightforward questions but has difficulty with some unexpected ones and needs some rephrasing. Fairly fluent, but some hesitation. <br> (b) Adequate range of structures and vocabulary. Can convey past and future meaning; some ambiguity. | 7–9 |
| Weak | (a) Has difficulty even with straightforward questions, but still attempts an answer. <br> (b) Shows elementary, limited vocabulary and faulty manipulation of structures. | 4–6 |
| Poor | (a) Frequently fails to understand the questions and has great difficulty in replying. <br> (b) Shows very limited range of structures and vocabulary. | 0–3 |

There are several observations to make before applying this scheme:
- It is based on *positive* achievement.
- If you have bilingual or exceptional candidates, do *not* consider their performance as the norm by which all others are to be judged. They are not typical FL learners.
- Start at the bottom of the bands and work upwards. If in doubt between two marks, go for the higher one – but be consistent in this practice.

- Do not mark your input. Some examiners tend to mark their own questions and give their candidates credit for what they have asked, rather than what they have answered!
- In scale (b), candidates cannot score above 6 if they cannot convey past and future meaning. (In training sessions we highlight the satisfactory marking band and use it as our starting point.)
- As linguists, we have often received a linguistic training ourselves which has focused on what is wrong rather than what is right. Remember that a candidate does not have to be error-free to access the higher mark bands.
- With good and able candidates, it is often the extent to which they can perform without your help that should guide you. The immediacy of response to a straightforward, or even a more unpredictable / less straightforward, question is a good indicator of ability.
- Work up through the mark bands until you reach one which is clearly beyond the performance, then go back down to check that the characteristics heard and observed are the best fit.
- Prepare to be surprised! Some candidates will achieve a different mark from the one you might have expected.

Remember that candidates *cannot* gain access to higher mark bands if the examiner merely asks straightforward questions, for example: 'What do you like to do at the weekend?' Responses to such questions rarely go beyond the actual. It is the response to 'Why?' questions that can push performances up. Likewise, avoid too many questions which demand only a 'Yes/No' response from candidates.

It can be seen, therefore, that although all candidates initially appear to do the same test their outcome in terms of performance may be totally different. The test caters for candidates of all abilities.

## How the examiner can get the best from candidates

The culmination of three, four or five years of language learning is for many students their 15-minute performance in the Speaking test. If we look at things from the candidate's point of view, what an ordeal this is: 15 minutes' preparation and then 15 minutes with their teacher/examiner – and it's recorded. Agony! (It could be, in the hands of an unsympathetic examiner.) It is also, frequently, the first formal external examination that they take. Even candidates displaying the greatest classroom bravado become anxious. How can we help?

The key to it all is de-mystifying the process and making candidates familiar with exactly *what* the test requires. It is therefore essential that examiners feel as competent as possible. If we do not prepare ourselves properly before the examination and if we are unclear about just what we examine, we will not give our candidates the best chance to achieve. Questions never asked cannot be answered. So the real issue to be addressed is: 'How do I get the best from my candidates, whatever their ability?'

## Preparation

Prepare your roles in the role plays. In the CIE IGCSE examination, for instance, you are allowed to have access to the materials up to four working days in advance of the test. The materials must remain in the centre in secure conditions, but you should arrange to familiarise yourself with exactly what the candidate has to do in each task. When examiners do not prepare fully, it is unfortunately the candidate who suffers. Know your role (and keep to it) so that you can perform your cues. This will help the candidate. If you are confident and relaxed, your candidate will be more confident.

## Asking the right questions

Success in the test depends on the examiner asking the right question. In the topic and general conversation sections, it is sometimes useful to use closed questions as starter questions, ones which demand only 'Yes' or 'No'. Generally, however, it is wiser to use a variety of question types and interrogative adverbs, from a basic level of simple questions which demand predictable, short responses to more searching questions such as 'Why?', 'Tell me about . . . ', 'What do you think about . . . ?' If candidates are clearly out of their depth with a question, feel free to rephrase it, but never correct them or leave them in a 'black hole' of silence. Likewise, feel free to change topics. With more able candidates, the avoidance of the more stretching question will mean that they do not do themselves justice.

## Using banks of questions

In the marking scheme, scale (a) refers to a hierarchy of questions which move from the simple, predictable questions with some unpredictable or unexpected elements, to unexpected questions which may require candidates to give reasons, explain and/or justify their opinions. One way in which teachers can prepare students during their course is to make use of banks of questions which tie in directly with the levels of performance featured in the marking bands. A popular activity in CIE IGCSE training courses is to devise such banks together. This could also form a useful activity in departmental meetings or on school training days. These banks can then be used in class during the teaching of related units.

Banks of questions can be given to students for use in class and as revision aids, but it is *not* recommended that they should be used in the test as the spontaneity of the situation is removed and candidates may sound very rehearsed. It is far better to familiarise candidates with topic areas during the course of study beforehand, and then to approach things more freely on the day. You need to give the candidate the opportunity to shape their response, not just to the expected question, but also at a higher level to the less predictable question.

The following questions are a suggested hierarchy that could be used to elicit different performances on the subject of holidays.

**Low-level questions**
Where do you go on holiday?
Where do you stay? In a hotel? At a campsite?
Describe the hotel, farm, house, and so on.
What do you do on holiday?
How long do you spend on holiday?
Who do you go with?
How do you travel?

**Higher-level questions**
These questions can be used alongside slightly more open question types.
Where did you go on holiday last year?
How did you travel?
Tell me about . . .
What did you do there?
What did you visit/eat/drink?
What was the hotel/campsite like?
What did you like best?
Do you want to go back? Why?
Give me an idea of a typical day on holiday.
What did you do when the weather was fine?
Where will you go on holiday next year?

**Questions at an even higher level**
These questions could be used to test the top bands of performance and could include more invitations to respond and more short questions of the 'Why?' variety which demand explanation and justification.
Did you like the way of life in . . . ? Why / Why not?
What differences did you notice between . . . and . . . ? (countries of choice)
Would you like to return to . . . ? Why / Why not?
Describe your ideal holiday. If you had the money where would you go?

Be aware, however, that at this level the 'Tell me about . . . ' questions should *not* be allowed to develop into a monologue. Also, remember that it is helpful to start candidates off with an easy question or two as a warm-up. One of the most frightening starts to a Speaking test would be 'Why do you think there is so much pollution?' Not only is the topic perceived by candidates to be hard, but it also makes use of 'Why?', which is, without doubt, an interrogative form usually answered well only by middle- to top-ability candidates.

### Guidance of candidates

Finally, tell the candidate in simple FL terms what you are doing as you progress through the test; for example, 'Fine, Cathy, we've finished the topic conversation; let's move on now to the general conversation. Let's talk about your school. Tell me about a typical school day . . . '.

Try to group the questions in topic areas. If you change topics, tell the candidate. The best performances from candidates of whatever ability come from situations in which the examiner leads them through the test clearly and actually listens to what they say!

## Conducting and assessing a Speaking test – practicalities

Every international centre I have visited has important local conditions to consider when organising Speaking tests. For these, long- and short-term planning is necessary. Remember the following things.

### In the long term

- Try to persuade your director / head of curriculum that you need practice Speaking tests (these are requirements equivalent to days out for coursework, which other faculties can require). Make the formality of these tests obvious to students – they need a practice run. It will also help you to respond to any problems that might occur later in the year.
- For these practice tests, persuade a senior staff member to give you their office for a day – it's quieter than a classroom. If possible, use a quiet area with a separate preparation area close by. Try to use a room where you will get the best possible sound quality.
- Your tape recorder should be serviced and then checked in the room where it is to be used.
- Remember to take phones off the hook, and try to be as far as possible from playgrounds and music practice rooms – especially if you are examining in a hot country, with no air conditioning and the windows open.
- Ask for a colleague to be free if possible to invigilate the preparation area. If not, a reliable senior student could be placed outside your door to act as a runner in case of problems.

## In the medium term (six weeks before)

- Timetable your students. Remember that you need 15 minutes to examine plus one or two minutes to complete marking, check the tape recorder and so on. Give them an arrival time and a time for the test itself.
- Work in blocks of four candidates when timetabling. Examining is tiring work which requires concentration. It is wise to build in a 5- or 10-minute break after every four or five candidates so that you can be fresh for the next set of candidates.
- Check your tape recorder (again).
- Check that students have prepared / are preparing their topic.

## In the short term (up to four days before the test)

- Prepare your materials.
- Fill in the mark-sheet details and make sure you have candidate numbers from the examinations officer as you will need to record them on the tape. Label tapes and boxes.
- Remind candidates that they must turn up on time and that they need to be out of class for 30 minutes. Remind them that dictionaries cannot be used in the preparation room.

## On the day

- Arrive early to set up your equipment (or set it up the previous evening). Remember, if you are using separate microphones, to plug them in and switch them on.
- Smile at the candidates as they come in – go and fetch each one and check that they have the same role play as you.
- Record all candidates – do not choose the six for your sample beforehand. They may surprise you on the day and you will not be able to make a true sample that reflects standards if they over-perform or under-perform. If you record everybody, it is fairer.
- Mark in the room – do not leave the marking to do afterwards. Your initial impression will be correct.
- Do not tell candidates how you think they have done as Centre marks have to be moderated by CIE and may be changed.
- If more than one examiner is used, complete a separate internal working mark sheet for each examiner. Candidate numbers and names must be clearly written. Candidates should be identified.

- Do not stop the tape at any point during a candidate's test. Recording should be continuous.
- Remember to take breaks. Keep a bottle of water in the room – it can be thirsty work.
- Have a stopwatch or clock to hand.

## Immediately after the test
- Make up your sample for the external moderator.
- If more than one examiner has been used, complete internal moderation (cross-mark each other) to check that all examiners have marked to the same standard.
- Check that all clerical work is correct. Check with the examinations officer that you have fulfilled the necessary requirements. Despatch the materials to CIE as soon as possible. (Pack the cassettes carefully.)
- Congratulate yourself!

You will receive feedback on the conduct and assessment of your candidates from CIE.

**LOOKING BACK**

- How useful do you feel the presentation–practice–communication model to be in terms of Speaking skills?
- To what extent are Speaking activities in your situation 'skill-getting' and 'skill-using'?
- What are the implications in the FL classroom of devising oral activities? Do your activities allow for pairwork?
- How can students be encouraged to move from supported to freer Speaking activities?
- To what extent do your students talk to each other in the TL? How best can such activities be encouraged?
- How best can you prepare for a summative Speaking test such as the CIE IGCSE Speaking test?
- What do you consider your role to be in a Speaking test? How can you get the best from candidates in the examination room?
- How is differentiation linked to questioning techniques and candidate performance?

# 6 Teaching and assessing Reading skills

Earlier chapters have highlighted the importance of an integrated skills approach within the Foreign Language (FL) classroom. Reading is crucial in this approach, but teachers often admit to having no real systematic programme to help students acquire Reading skills. It is perhaps the skill that is least taught formally – we sometimes expect our learners to absorb the written word as if by magic.

Reading is frequently seen as a passive skill, in that it is a receptive rather than productive skill. But, for reading to have meaning, readers need to be active in the learning process – they need to be able to relate to and understand the text, and this is an interactive process. Reading for interest or pleasure may be the final aim, but it is important to consider the hierarchy of skills necessary in the reading process to help our readers acquire confidence and autonomy.

Likewise, within the testing situation, reading underpins all the assessment objectives. Students need to be able to read role-play stimuli and access questions on Listening and Writing papers through their Reading skills.

This chapter will examine the hierarchical nature of Reading Comprehension skills and will consider the skills that students need to cope with the different kinds of texts they encounter. The final section of the chapter relates these teaching objectives to the assessment objectives of the CIE IGCSE examination, and surveys the question types frequently used within the testing situation.

## What are Reading Comprehension skills?
### 'Bottom-up' and 'top-down' skills
Reading skills are often regarded as receptive skills and likened to Listening skills. There are similarities, but one important difference is that the reader can take control of the input more easily. A Listening input is often taped with pauses built in or controlled by a teacher. When reading

solo, however, the reader determines the speed of the activity. This is one positive thing to stress to students.

Like Listening skills, Reading skills can be seen in terms of 'bottom-up' and 'top-down' skills. Bottom-up (or systemic) skills consist of building up meaning from analysing the form of the language used (e.g. from words to clauses to sentences to paragraphs). A text may be partially understood at this level, but it is unlikely that a full understanding can be achieved without top-down skills. Top-down (or schematic) skills involve the prior world knowledge brought by the reader to the text. This kind of knowledge can be seen as being cultural or world knowledge. Our learners therefore need both types of skill if they are to make sense of a text, and our methodology needs to pay attention to both.

Bottom-up skills of language knowledge enable readers to work closely on a text, decoding words, structures and other linguistic features. A fluent reader, as Hedge (2000: 192) says, 'has a good knowledge of language structures and can recognise a wide range of vocabulary automatically'. It follows that, alongside a structured programme of new linguistic features, a major strategy to help students is to find ways of enabling them to acquire vocabulary. If a text has a very high density of unknown words, it is very off-putting for readers. This, in turn, suggests that, before students encounter a new text in class, the teacher needs to present any new lexical items and/or structures. **Pre-reading** tasks such as vocabulary games, wordsearches and matching synonyms can all help students to approach a text in a more confident way. The noting down of new vocabulary according to topic areas may not be the latest idea in the FL world, but it is certainly not one to be scorned. The greater the degree of prior knowledge, the greater the degree of automatic response the reader has to a text – which in turn will help confidence levels.

Other pre-reading activities that can help readers relate to the full meaning of a text are ones which activate top-down skills, or schematic knowledge. Certain words may activate prior knowledge in a reader – for example, references to pop-star culture, film stars, sports, travel and school experience. It is helpful to discuss what the content of a text may be from looking at its title, headlines and photos. If we activate our students' ability to predict and guess, we are already taking away some of the difficulty of the text. This, again, has implications for our choice of texts. It is important to choose a text to which our readers can relate in terms of content and maturity. Likewise, the layout, size of font and use of photos can be appealing or off-putting.

- Choose a text based on a topic you are teaching to an examination class. Think of pre-reading strategies that activate both bottom-up and top-down skills.
- Consider a text which one of your classes has found accessible. List the reasons why it has worked.
- Consider the nature not just of the text, but of the tasks based on it. Can the same text be used with different levels of learners if the tasks are changed?

## How is reading purposeful?

It is acknowledged (Hedge 2000: 195) that readers need to use different subskills to deal with different kinds of text. A reader will also use different subskills according to the reason for reading. These subskills are as follows:

- **Receptive** – reading a short story or article for enjoyment.
- **Reflective** – episodes of reading interspersed with pauses for reflection and re-reading.
- **Scanning** – rapid searching through a text to find a specific point of information.
- **Intensive** – reading which involves close detail and looking carefully at a text (e.g. a poem) in order to appreciate it.

These subskills involve both top-down (schematic) and bottom-up (systemic) skills. It would perhaps be very difficult to discuss in the Target Language (TL) the nature of these skills with students, but it may well be worth explaining to them in their mother tongue or common working language just how these skills work.

The different types of skills, especially scanning and skimming, are very relevant at O Level and GCSE, and it can really help students if they appreciate that they do not need to know every word in a text in order to complete Reading tasks well.

### Teacher activity 6.2

Study the four Reading subskills and identify which ones involve bottom-up skills and which ones involve top-down skills.

## A hierarchy of Reading activities

Lussier (1993: 115) groups the kinds of Reading Comprehension activities used for testing purposes. This also serves as a good checklist within the teaching situation. They are given in a hierarchical order as follows:

- **Locate** – identify, recognise, select . . . one or several elements of information already present in a text.
- **Reorganise** – classify, order information explicitly present in a text.
- **Compare** – distinguish, associate . . . information with a view to extracting similarities or differences present in one or several texts.
- **Infer** – deduce, predict, interpret, extrapolate . . . the information contained explicitly as a function of the text.
- **Appreciate** – distinguish a fact from an opinion or feeling . . . evaluate the correctness of a piece of information: judge whether an action is good or bad.

When trying to gauge how difficult a particular text will be for students, we need to bear in mind not only the inherent difficulty of the text, but also the nature of the tasks we plan to set and whether we require students to attempt such tasks before, during or after they have studied the text.

- **Pre-reading tasks.** Such tasks (as discussed earlier in this chapter) enable students to familiarise themselves with the content of a text. Activities can be systemic (such as vocabulary exercises) or schematic (such as thinking of the purpose of a text or predicting the content from its title).
- **While-reading tasks.** These kinds of task, as Hedge (2000: 210) states, have become more used: 'since the adoption of the idea of reading as an interactive process . . . these encourage learners to be active as they read. Students can be given activities which require them to do any of the following: follow the order of ideas in a text; react to the opinions expressed; understand the information it contains; ask themselves questions; make notes; confirm expectations of prior knowledge or predict the next part of a text from various clues.'
- **Post-reading tasks.** These tasks follow up the work covered and seek to extend candidates. Such activities are Directed Writing activities, or role-play and group discussion activities.

All the above kinds of activity can be undertaken on an individual or group basis. Reading is frequently thought of as being a solo, 'quiet' activity, but group pre- and post-reading activities can motivate the crucial while-reading activities. It is also useful to set a time limit for while-reading activities to keep readers on task and to be able to move on to post-reading activities as a group.

Choose a text from a coursebook you use with a final-year class. Think of pre-reading and post-reading activities that you could link to the text. Consider whether the activities are better undertaken solo or in groups. Finally, remember that pre-reading and post-reading activities could be linked into other language skills such as Listening and Writing. Coursebooks often feature this multiskills approach so that the skills reinforce each other.

## Free reading as a way to learner autonomy

Surely the greatest motivating force for our students is reading for pleasure. The activities we have mentioned thus far will probably be chosen by the teacher as part of a structured programme of learning. But how often do we let students choose their own reading matter? Indeed, do we encourage them to read extensively? Are they ever free just to sit and read, as I have frequently seen English students do in English classtime? Perhaps it is our task as FL teachers to go beyond coursebooks and to introduce our students to a challenging element of the Target Language (TL) which can add a new dimension to their learning and which can give them some autonomy.

## Creating the right conditions in which to 'free read'

One of the most inspiring classrooms I have visited featured a reading corner. There were three or four comfortable chairs and low tables covered with foreign teenage magazines, graded readers on shelves and topic-based files filled with interesting articles graded by difficulty. There were also several computers linked to the school network. Students were allowed to access the corner during lunchtimes and also in designated reading time during classtime, when activities were non-teacher-led. All the students had a record card on which to note what they had read and give their comments in the TL on each book or magazine. They could also use this mini-library to borrow publications to take home. Although a resource of this kind is not achieved overnight, there are points of good practice to note which could be achieved fairly easily over several years:

- If finances do not permit a reading corner, set aside an area of shelving so that materials are on show, not hidden away in cupboards.
- If students visit a TL country, encourage them to bring back magazines.
- Using simple coloured stickers, code the front covers of magazines to indicate the level of difficulty or the year for which it is appropriate.
- Involve your school librarian (and, if possible, library funds).
- Persuade your school library to purchase a good set of graded readers. Some coursebooks have linked graded readers for younger readers,

and many FL publishers in the UK now have materials that look far more authentic in nature. The topics chosen should, ideally, reflect what the average teenager is interested in and be expressed in language of an appropriate level.

- Try to subscribe to at least one teenage FL magazine. (Searching the Internet is a good way to seek out publishers' details and titles.)
- Storage does not have to be elegant. Plastic boxes will do, but try to store magazines by title and category of interest.
- Make sure that all learners keep a record card of what they have read and that they make simple comments on its content (such as 'Super!', 'Interesting!', 'Boring!'). A star-rating system can be used. Older learners can be asked to write simple critical appreciations for younger learners, which could go on the wall round the reading area.
- The record card system works better if the teacher ticks off the titles read. This ensures some form of monitoring.
- Keep a variety of reading material. Students love comic-strip books, animal books, short-story books, books on sport, computers and celebrities.
- Do not be overambitious for your students. Tell them to progress from easy to hard and to read different kinds of publications. Make them aware of how the system of coding works. This obviously means that you and your colleagues need to do some initial grading of content and linguistic suitability of materials.
- Reading for pleasure is not suddenly 'caught' in the last two years of study. Introduce students in younger years – it is a habit which can be learned.
- Persuade older learners to write short stories or poems for younger learners – they will provide language at a lower level and have a good idea of how to interest younger learners.
- Remember that the Internet has sites linked to teenage FL magazines. Let students browse through these. Keep a list of good, suitable sites to visit. Students should include these on their record cards.
- Tell your learners that reading for pleasure is a calm, reflective activity upon which they need to concentrate. Students (and teachers) live in noisy surroundings – it is good to temper loud group activities with periods of calm.
- Tell your students that they do not need to understand every word – they are reading for gist initially. Do keep dictionaries in the reading area, however, so that they can check difficult vocabulary.
- Explain thoroughly how the system will work – do not just let them have access to a pile of ungraded materials as that will demotivate them.
- Encourage, persuade and – most of all – give practice in reading by allowing the time, even if it is only 15 minutes a week.

- Consider the advantages of setting up a reading scheme in your school. What would your first-year targets be?
- Consider the advantages/disadvantages of linking questions/activities to free reading. Why would you be for or against this?

## Linking the teaching and assessment objectives

The CIE IGCSE scheme of assessment features an Integrated Skills Paper (Paper 2) which tests both Reading and Directed Writing. There are, however, distinct sections of the paper which are designed specifically to test Reading Comprehension skills. In these Reading questions, the way in which a candidate writes is *not* assessed in terms of quality of language. If the candidate clearly communicates the message and demonstrates understanding, the mark is scored. (The Writing tasks are assessed in a different way – see Chapter 7.)

## Core Reading skills

The CIE IGCSE syllabus curriculum content states that Core students should be able to:

- demonstrate understanding of words within short texts such as public notices, instructions and signs
- extract relevant specific information from texts, such as brochures, guides, letters and forms of imaginative writing, considered likely to be within the experience of, and reflecting the interests of, young people
- show a general understanding of more extended texts
- scan for particular information, organise the relevant information and present it in a given format.

This gives important indications of the textual input likely to be encountered by candidates. These textual inputs can be linked back to Lussier's (1993) hierarchy of Reading activities in that the above four objectives correspond to the skills of locating, reorganising and comparing. The Reading subskills most involved when meeting such texts would be scanning and skimming. Within the first section of the test, the topics and vocabulary featured in the texts and questions are drawn from areas A, B and C of the *Defined Content* booklets.

As in Listening tests, within the testing context it is important to view the difficulty of an exercise not just in terms of text, but also in terms of task. Candidates are deliberately set a variety of question types. Great attention is paid to the wording of the questions to ensure that the comprehension of the question does not become too much of a test in itself. Some of the question types frequently used are as follows:

- Objective
  - multiple choice (with or without visuals), candidate chooses one option
  - box-ticking
  - matching exercises
  - grid-filling
  - true/false (ticking)
  - gap-filling.
- Non-objective (especially on longer texts)
  - short answers in the TL (full sentences not required)
  - correction of an incorrect statement.

Modern coursebooks frequently feature these question types. Students would be well advised to study the sorts of rubric they will meet in the examination so that they feel at ease with the format of the question.

## Extended Reading skills

All candidates attempt Sections 1 and 2 of Paper 2 and, for the more able students, additional assessment objectives are tested in Section 3. These objectives go beyond the comprehension of the factual and the understanding of opinions. For Section 3 candidates should be able to:

- show comprehension of a wider range of texts, including magazines and newspapers likely to be read by young people
- demonstrate the ability to identify the important point or themes within an extended piece of writing
- draw conclusions from, and see relations within, an extended text.

The whole of the CIE IGCSE Reading and Directed Writing paper features an incline of difficulty, and the above objectives are clearly more demanding than those for Sections 1 and 2. Texts are longer and require a more sophisticated appreciation and response from candidates. Questions test both general and specific understanding, and the most demanding questions will require candidates to draw conclusions and make inferences. In essence, they should go beyond 'What?' questions and be able to answer 'Why?' questions.

It is important to emphasise to students that when they respond in the TL, especially for longer texts in Section 3, they must not content themselves with 'lifting' large chunks of the text, including material irrelevant to the question, as it is unlikely that this will show comprehension. In terms of teaching strategies, it is well worth teaching students to use synonyms by providing in class examples of new vocabulary items with equally valid alternatives such as, in French, *nager* and *faire de la natation.*

## Teacher activity 6.5

- Compare the types of Reading tasks in your coursebook to the types of task encountered in a CIE IGCSE / O Level Reading paper. Does the coursebook offer a range of text and task type?
- Consider the Section 3 objectives. Consider what kinds of linguistic expressions students might need to be able to compare, contrast and express preferences. Try to design a worksheet to revise such expressions.

## LOOKING BACK

- ◆ How can the student become more active in the reading process?
- ◆ How useful is it to have an understanding of bottom-up (systematic) and top-down (schematic) approaches to Reading skills?
- ◆ Which subskills are needed by readers to deal with different kinds of text? Which ones are relevant to your teaching situation?
- ◆ How does free reading promote learner autonomy? What initial steps would you take to set up a reading-for-pleasure scheme?
- ◆ What have you learnt about the importance of a gradient of difficulty in Reading exercises in the examination context?
- ◆ Which question and exercise types do you consider to be best suited to testing Reading Comprehension?

# 7 Teaching and assessing Writing skills

The development of communicative competence depends on a multiskill approach in the classroom. It is, however, important to focus on the skill of Writing, as it is a skill that is both complementary and crucial to responding to other inputs such as Listening and Reading. Traditionally, in many countries and many pedagogies, it was considered to be the predominant skill, and in some countries this is still very much the case.

It is necessary, therefore, to address the issue of how much importance we now, as FL teachers, place upon the ability of our students to write. Do we place more emphasis on writing accurately or do we emphasise the importance of conveying a message? How do we mark written work and, perhaps more importantly, how do we help our students to become involved in the process of writing? Do we always look for a finished end product, or are we active in helping them to become involved in the craft of writing – which emphasises the process and the acquisition of skills that make a good writer? Indeed, what makes a good writer at this level of learning?

Traditionally, FL teaching placed emphasis on a grammar, translation and essay-writing approach. This was reflected in assessment objectives and testing. Things have, however, evolved. This chapter will explore the CIE IGCSE assessment objectives and relate the teaching to the testing.

Students themselves often attach differing levels of importance to the skill of Writing. This can sometimes depend on the importance given to Writing within both their mother tongue and their local context. In some countries, Writing is still seen as the most important skill and, due to their learning experiences in other areas of the curriculum, students often perceive Writing to be the most important skill, as they 'do a lot of writing' in other lessons. A tangible end product is often a reward in itself. This is not counterproductive for FL teaching, but within a multiskill approach in the FL classroom we should emphasise that students need to acquire a sense of purpose and audience in their writing, and that it is one of four interdependent skills that reinforce the whole experience of FL acquisition.

This chapter will examine the nature of Writing skills in the FL context, together with ways of encouraging such skills in our learners. The importance of feedback and ways of correcting written work will be explored, and these, in turn, will be contextualised within the CIE IGCSE scheme of assessment for Writing.

## The hierarchy of Writing skills

Traditionally, Writing has been perceived as a hard skill at which to excel for many of our learners. In the past, tasks set did not relate to the students' own experience or needs. As methodology moved on from the late 1980s, there came a shift of emphasis away from third-person descriptions to different styles of writing, demanding a personal response in the first person (e.g. informal and formal letters). Students were required to think of the purpose of their writing within a communicative context and of their audience.

In the past, coursebook materials were frequently based on a Listening, Speaking, Reading, Writing approach. As Cajkler and Addelman (2000: 40) say, 'The result could often be that writing was relegated to the end of the lesson, largely devoted to copying down models of language.' Instead, they consider, it is more helpful to view Writing not just as an end activity in the process of skills acquisition, but in terms of how 'all the skills fit into the process of language learning on the principle of gradually diminishing support'.

So, what are the stages of learning through which a typical FL writer will pass? At the beginning of the process, one should wait until new lexical items have been heard and seen – Writing has to be introduced as a support for the other skills. Indeed, in my own experience of once trying to teach beginners for six weeks without their writing at all, I found they were simply hiding notebooks under their desks and writing down phonetic transcriptions of sorts! Students *need* to write as part of the all-round process of language acquisition.

Different forms of Writing on the continuum ranging from support to independence and free writing can be seen in the following hierarchies.

## Practice activities
- **Copying phrases, matching phrases to pictures.**
- **Unjumbling sentences.** Students sort out mixed-up sentences. The teacher can insist on accuracy as learners become more proficient.
- **Gap-filling.** This can serve not only as an exercise in reading for meaning, but also as an aid to heighten students' awareness of grammatical forms. The exercise can be made easier by providing options from which students choose.

- **Completion of phrases.** This can be viewed in two ways. Teachers can expect students to complete phrases in order to test vocabulary and/or grammatical accuracy.
- **Substitution.** This can be in the form of a guided model with underlined items which students have to replace in order to generate a different final product.

## Production activities
- **Writing short linked sentences.** Examples are short answers to TL questions, short poems, and eventually short messages (e.g. postcards, messages, short paragraphs).
- **Writing e-mails and word processing short pieces.**
- **Writing short letters.** Writing formal and informal letters, making use of paragraphs within a very guided framework – such as responding to very directed tasks/questions within a stimulus letter (or memo or fax).
- **Writing longer letters and texts (e.g. articles).** Writing of a more personal nature, for which less initial guidance is given.
- **Writing descriptive paragraphs.** Writing paragraphs that go beyond factual information.
- **Writing descriptive, free accounts.** These are accounts that narrate events, in which students can show the ability to go beyond the factual by giving and justifying their opinions and describing their reactions to events.

### Teacher activity 7.1

- Think of a beginners' FL class you teach. Which kinds of practice and production activities do you use both in and out of the classroom?
- To what extent do your students write in class and out of class? Does Writing tend to be a homework activity, or do you see it as a process which supports the learning of the other skills in class?
- Think of a class in the final two years of FL learning. Devise one practice and one production activity that would be appropriate to a topic you are currently teaching. Can you set the same task for all students, or do you need to set differentiated tasks if you have a mixed-ability group?
- Do you think that production activities can be set for all the classes you teach? If yes, why is this important?

Much early Writing in the FL classroom may be undertaken as an aid to learning (practice activities), but it is important to remember that in the early stages learners can often feel frustrated if they have few opportunities to make real use of the language in order to communicate. Such opportunities are needed to maintain their motivation and interest. It is highly relevant therefore to think of the approach we take to the evaluation of written work, and whether we reward content or form or both. This will be discussed later in the chapter.

## Setting the parameters for Writing tasks

Hedge (2000: 8–12) refers to the necessity to establish a framework for successful Writing, and there are seven fundamental assumptions underlying this framework. She refers to the role of teachers in building **communicative** potential.

### Assumption 1
Based on the need for writers to write **whole texts** of a connected **communicative** nature.

### Assumption 2
Students need to practise various **forms** and **functions**, based on a list of skills that writers need (Hedge 1988: 8), which are:
- getting the grammar right
- having a range of vocabulary
- punctuating meaningfully
- using the conventions of layout correctly, e.g. in letters
- spelling accurately
- using a range of sentence structures
- linking ideas and information across sentences to develop a topic
- developing and organising the content clearly and convincingly.

### Assumption 3
Emphasises the need to encourage students to go through a process of **planning**, **organising**, **composing** and **revising**. Hedge sees good writers as 'people who have a sense of purpose, a sense of audience, and a sense of direction in their writing' (Hedge 1988: 10).

### Assumption 4
Refers to the need for teachers to set tasks with a **sense of purpose** (Why am I doing this task?) and a **sense of audience** (For whom?). This underlines the need for us as teachers to create a purposeful context when setting Writing tasks.

## Assumption 5

Concerned with **marking** (see below for further treatment of approaches to marking). Marking was traditionally based on indicating errors and taking marks off. As methodology has evolved, there is now a much more positive emphasis, on marking what is right. Perhaps more importantly (I speak as one who has produced kilometres of red ink on books), we should be involving students more in assessing not only their own work but also that of their peers. If students can learn ways of marking their work, it can become, as Hedge says, 'part of the writing process and a genuine source of learning' (Hedge 1988: 10).

## Assumption 6

This underlines the importance of affording students the time to write in class. All too frequently, poor writers do not write enough and become even less motivated to write. Many students write independently more frequently out of class as a homework activity because teachers often want to focus on Speaking/Listening activities in the classroom. There is, however, a strong argument for setting aside time in class during which teachers and students can focus on planning, drafting and revising. In this way, the process of writing is supported **actively**, and poorer writers especially may feel more confident about writing independently.

## Assumption 7

Collaborative Writing in class encourages an effective process of writing. Hedge advocates group composition, during which students work together in small groups on a Writing task. Various activities, such as brainstorming a topic in a group to produce ideas and points of language, followed by organising ideas logically, are put forward. A group first draft is then produced with one student acting as a scribe. Other students are expected to 'argue out structures, sentences and the choice of words' (Hedge 1988: 12). However, there is a danger that the strongest in a group can take over, so the balance of input from different group members needs to be monitored carefully by teachers. Collaborative Writing can be very fruitful. In my own experience, it has worked best when an initial class brainstorm (perhaps using a class mind map on the board) focuses first on content (ideas, linking of ideas) and then on the language (phrases needed, etc). Groups then take responsibility for different paragraphs or parts of a letter or account. A final group activity assembles the efforts of the different groups, and a final model is achieved. The class is invited to comment and review the whole. This can be an end product in itself or, after a time for study, the model can be withdrawn and students asked to produce their own version in class, with further assistance if necessary from the teacher.

This idea of Collaborative Writing sits well within the framework of diminishing support and actually involves students in the process of writing. It also aids students who have poor composing competence. Weak writers tend to get bogged down on smaller chunks of language, and often fail to see the importance of the whole task and the necessity to get complete ideas down. Students need to be encouraged to link ideas together. They then need to be encouraged to return to their ideas and reformulate their work in terms of improving the language. Redrafting and reformulation are important Writing skills. If you have access to IT and word-processing facilities, this approach can work well; but it is one that can work equally well with pen and paper, and it affords support to the learner who may often feel daunted by their inability to express their ideas owing to linguistic shortcomings. Collaborative classwork can give great support on both a linguistic and a conceptual level. Learners can be encouraged to think about purpose and audience, and the skill of planning – too often neglected by students – can be emphasised.

## Approaches to marking

In the late 1980s approaches to marking written work within the examination context underwent a groundshift. Until then, it is fair to say that evaluating work was largely a question of pointing out errors in terms of linguistic content. The magical 20 out of 20 or an A was elusive as marks always ended up being deducted. Marking often emphasised what was wrong, rather than rewarding what was right.

As the emphasis on communicative methodology gained importance, a new emphasis in marking came about. This was not, as some would mistakenly think, a matter of ignoring error, but a question of rewarding what students could get right – not just in linguistic terms but in terms of communicative content. It was seen to be important to reward students if they were successful in terms of transmitting messages, as well as rewarding them with extra marks if they were able to communicate these ideas in a way which was accurate.

It is by no means the intention of this book to advocate one particular method for your students. For some, it is a major achievement to be able to convey simple ideas which answer the set tasks. Others should easily be able to go beyond basic communication and should aim to convey ideas accurately. Whatever the level of student, all teachers want to help them improve.

With my own examination classes, I mark students' independent written work for both communication and accuracy. In the case of weaker learners, I have sometimes marked just for communication. Ticks are placed on what is good. I have evolved a system of underlining errors and placing a mark in the margin, such as *V* (verb) or *T* (tense). I do not always feel the need to correct the incorrect form for the student. This is contentious! Indeed, the word for marking in many different languages is 'correction'. But, should it *always* be the teacher who corrects? Students can be made to think far more analytically about error and how to rectify it if incorrect structures are indicated, but not corrected by the teacher. This approach does however rely on all students being made aware of the abbreviations used and of their responsibility to check and try to self-correct. The teacher then reviews their corrections, either on the spot in a 5-minute correction/help session, or when the student's book is next seen.

One method that can work well in terms of evaluating and giving feedback is that of peer correction. It is possible to indicate clearly the communicative tasks to be covered and to ask students to read the work of others and place a tick for each idea communicated. Likewise, a certain amount of positive marking can be done at a linguistic level. Students can, for example, be asked to indicate one good feature of language (e.g. correct use of a past tense or adverbial time phrase) in a whole piece of work. They often enjoy this and, more importantly, they read the work of others with care even if they neglect their own. By reinforcing what is correctly communicated or accurately expressed, marking can take on a different dimension for the student. It is far more rewarding to see ticks (even if mistakes are underlined) than to see nothing on a piece of writing except the underlining of errors and lots of red corrections. It is, of course, important for the teacher to conduct a group feedback on common errors before inviting individual comment. Finally, within this context, it is important to decide on an appropriate marking strategy for an individual or group piece of work.

### Teacher activity 7.2

Try to devise a Writing task for final-year students that could be marked positively for both communication and accuracy. Work out:
- how many marks you would allocate to each category;
- how you would indicate success (e.g. communication ticks in the left-hand margin and correct language ticks over each structure);
- how much correct usage you would indicate (e.g. all verbs);
- how you would indicate areas for further attention (i.e. incorrect language) – try to be as positive as possible.

Remember, many linguists worldwide have one common experience. Many of us have come through systems where error was indicated, but not success. It is our duty to help students to improve, and the more we help them to focus on their success, both in terms of content and language, the more their motivation will increase.

## Writing assessment objectives

The CIE IGCSE syllabus for FL states the Core Writing objectives as follows:

> carry out basic writing tasks (such as asking for detailed information, giving some personal information, reporting).

Paper 2, Reading and Directed Writing, features two Writing tasks that are common to all candidates, whether Core or Extended. The first rewards candidates 'more for their skill in communicating a message than the extent to which they are accurate. Material that is irrelevant to the set tasks does not score marks. Minus marks are *never* used: candidates are given every opportunity to gain marks for what they can do.'

A typical example of this first task is the writing of a message, note or postcard. Visuals can be given to help cue responses. There are 5 marks available (of which 3 would be rewards for communication and 2 for appropriateness of language). This Writing task is aimed at lower-level learners (grades E, F, G).

The second Writing task carries 10 marks for communication, and 5 for quality of language. The syllabus states clearly that this is a Directed Writing task. Candidates have to write a simple letter of up to a hundred words. Again, communication marks are seen to be more important at this level, with 10 of the 15 marks being awarded for relevant answers to the tasks outlined in the question. There are 5 marks available for the quality of language. These are based on correctly used units of language such as subject and verb, preposition and verb, and so on. Examiners seek material worthy of credit and do *not* indicate error. This is an approach that complements the evolution seen in methodology. What is done well is rewarded. Candidates are rewarded for what they know and can do. Exercises at this level would typically be responding to a penfriend on topics such as school, home life, interests or perhaps holidays, and they target the kind of language that one could expect from candidates in a C–D range of grades.

## Extended Writing skills

The CIE IGCSE candidate who wishes to have access to the highest grades (A*–B) is expected to sit Paper 4 (Continuous Writing). This paper requires candidates to produce two pieces of Continuous Writing in which 'they demonstrate their mastery of the written language in a more "open" way than in the written tasks on the Reading and Directed Writing paper. At this level, candidates are expected to express thoughts, feelings and opinions and to narrate events in the past and to demonstrate control of vocabulary, syntax and grammar, punctuation and spelling.'

Again, a system of positive marking is used. Each piece of writing is marked out of 25, and 15 of these marks are available for accuracy / quality of language. It is important to reward more able candidates not just for their ability to communicate (for which 5 marks are available) but also for doing so in an accurate way, and to allow them to show that they can go beyond the factual and use more adventurous language. The 5 marks that are available also for general impression encourage candidates to use a range of structures and lexis. At this level, the hallmark of a good performance is the ability to communicate accurately in a variety of timeframes and to use subordination.

Although it is not possible to provide details of the Writing mark schemes for all the CIE IGCSE FL syllabuses here, it is important to underline the fact that they all share a positive approach.

## Teacher activity 7.3

- Using past CIE IGCSE question papers, set two Extended Writing tasks appropriate to your teaching groups, and try to use a positive marking scheme which reflects the approach used in the CIE IGCSE scheme of assessment.
- What problems do you envisage if you were to use this approach on a daily basis? Is it more suited to assessment only, or could you adapt it to daily use? If so, what adaptations would you make?

 **LOOKING BACK**

- ◆ To what extent are the Writing activities of your learners 'practice' or 'production' activities?
- ◆ How do you evaluate written work? Do you ever use positive marking schemes? Could you include positive evaluation in your teaching and learning activities?
- ◆ Review the seven assumptions (Hedge 2000: 8–12) and evaluate their relevance to your own teaching situation. How can you enable your students to plan, draft and revise Writing tasks? Is it feasible in your context to carry out collaborative Writing tasks?
- ◆ Consider your Writing marking schemes. Do they emphasise communication and/or accuracy? Do you use different schemes for learners of different abilities?

# 8 ICT in Foreign Language teaching

Foreign Languages (FL) teachers are always anxious to integrate good resources and ideas into their teaching programmes. Technology has provided us with a wealth of new resources to improve both the quality of our teaching and the students' learning experience.

ICT provision varies enormously in the international context. Some schools may have fully networked access, some schools may have no provision – or very little, due to financial constraints. Likewise, some teachers may have access to ICT at home but not at school. Finally, some teachers are very ICT literate and others may not have yet had the opportunity to taste what is on offer. This chapter aims to give a brief introduction and overview of the opportunities offered by ICT, and gives some useful sites for further exploration.

## ICT: an overview

Many teachers, if they are honest, approach the use of ICT with mixed feelings. To non-specialists it can seem a little intimidating, especially if you have not received some form of training. But the important thing to remember is that ICT constitutes not an end in itself but another tool at our disposal to help learners of FL.

> New Media are not seen as a panacea for teaching/learning problems, nor are they a replacement for present models of language learning — ICT alone cannot provide a comprehensive basis for language learning. ICT must be integrated into present, proven and successful practice if full benefits of their advantages are to be reaped. (Davies, G. 2003)

Cajkler and Addelman (2000: 171) cite the potential of this teaching aid as being significant in many ways:

- It motivates pupils of all abilities.
- It enables pupils to work independently and away from the teacher.

- Disruptive pupils are often calmed by computers and work better.
- Teachers can create tasks based on the four skills.

The role of the teacher in this learning context shifts from a didactic one to that of facilitator. This implies that the learning experience is shared, and that both teachers and learners need to have certain ICT basics to enable students to access information.

Before taking whole groups into an ICT suite, it is important to be familiar with the technology and useful to have a reliable and able student to help you manage the system (and always have a Plan B in case the technology fails). Different classroom dynamics prevail in an ICT suite, and this also brings up issues such as the use of the Target Language (TL). It is important, if you are trying to make maximum use of the TL, that students first have knowledge of frequently used ICT expressions. (See the reference to BECTA in the Professional development section on page 85 for TL lists of such expressions.) It is also essential to realise that the constraints of being timetabled for a whole period in the ICT room may be inappropriate – the computer may be needed only to complete one or two tasks in your lesson objectives. Tasks to be achieved need to be integrated into a sound lesson plan so that the ICT becomes a tool for learning and not the main aim in itself. It is important to give students a clear expectation of what you expect them to have achieved by the end of the lesson.

## Information retrieval

One of the most common uses of ICT is information retrieval. Making use of the Internet and web-based resources offers access to a huge and dynamic range of authentic multimedia materials. In this respect, the language coursebook is no longer the only source of information available to the student. Multimedia programmes offer sound and vision showing how native speakers use the TL. Students can access a wide variety of web sites, such as web sites created by students in foreign countries, online newspapers (e.g. www.lemonde.fr), TV and radio stations, sports results and weather reports. If your students enter the Internet via a search engine such as Google (which offers access in many languages), they can easily access the richness of information available on the web. However, this can be a problem as they may be tempted to surf the web too freely without any real aim. It is important, therefore, to help students to develop their critical ability in terms of sifting the relevant from the irrelevant.

It is useful to talk to your ICT technical support team in school and ask if they can set up a Languages area within your local area network, where you can store downloaded offline versions of web sites *you* wish pupils to access. Also, if you have only a slow connection to the Internet, this will allow all the class to access these sites without unreasonable waiting times. If you have such a Languages area, students could also use it to post their work for peer review, to exchange ideas and to share information with each other.

## E-mail

E-mail is widely used in the FL context. It provides extended opportunities for interacting with the language and culture of the respective TL community worldwide. Contact can be made through e-mail and to a growing degree by videoconferencing and discussion groups. Students can now send and receive text, sound, image and video files. The potential for group work and project work with a partner school in a TL country is great. Partner-finding services on the Internet include ePals Classroom Exchange (available at www.epals.com) and Windows on the World (www.wotw.org.uk). Pachler and Field (2002) cite several case studies of using e-mail links in their very useful chapter on the use of ICT in FL teaching and learning. Townsend (1997) also offers guidance on the use of e-mail in FL teaching, listing topics which can be drawn upon, such as:

- pocket money;
- pop music;
- meals/food;
- our town;
- news comment;
- holidays;
- jobs;
- book reviews;
- captions for cartoons;
- sports.

## Software

Initially, in the 1980s and 1990s, software was limited very much to what could be defined as 'drill and kill'. As Davies, G. (2002) points out, the early gap-filling and multiple-choice exercises have now been replaced by an ever-expanding array of programmes such as:

- reordering exercises;
- text manipulation;
- word games;
- action mazes;
- simulations;
- adventures;
- discovery and exploration programmes;
- Guided Writing programmes;
- Reading Comprehension exercises – including timed reading;
- Listening exercises;
- building a personal database (e.g. vocabulary and grammar);
- e-mail activities.

Jones (1986), however, rightly points out: 'It's not so much the program, more what you do with it.'

As with any teacher resource, software has to be integrated into an all-round plan of attack and requires teacher imagination. Software nowadays offers the possibility of different levels of interactivity with students, and has the added advantage that immediate feedback can be given to students – which is highly motivating. Many new language coursebooks have accompanying CD-ROMs which are more sophisticated than traditional media. If you have a CD-ROM player, soundcard, headphones and/or speakers, you will find a wealth of exciting new materials is now available. But, where does one start? It can be daunting. The essential point to consider is whether it is appropriate for purpose or will remain unused on a shelf. Can it do what a book can't?

The evaluation of materials is important. It is not appropriate here to recommend language-specific software, given the generic approach of this book, but sources to search for suitable software do exist. The web site www.curriculumonline.gov.uk provides a search engine for thousands of commercially available resources related to the English National Curriculum, organised by subject and age range. Module 1.2 on the ICT4LT web site (www.ict4lt.org) – 'Introduction to computer hardware and software: what the language teacher needs to know' – also provides an excellent introduction (if a little dated in parts) to some of the slightly more technical issues surrounding hardware and software, and is a good source of knowledge to help you evaluate ICT-based resources.

## Word processing

Like information retrieval, word processing is one of the more widely used applications of ICT in the FL classroom. Hewer (1992; and in module 1.1 of the ICT4LT web site) refers to 'flexible' text. The essential nature of all word processors, whether simple or complex, is the provisional nature of the text generated. It is this which differentiates word-processed text from traditionally written or spoken forms. There need never be a final version. The potential for making changes has considerable implications for FL learners, some of whom in the past have found the development of Writing skills in the TL a less than happy and successful experience. Text produced using a pen and paper becomes a fixed object which can be criticised but which can only be corrected, often in a piecemeal way, by rubbing out, crossing out or rewriting. The activity is oriented towards failure from the outset since, in the students' eyes, errors detected by the teacher denote failure (Hewer 1992).

As text produced by word processing is provisional, learners can draft, review, edit, revise and redraft. Learners can write together, and 'shared Writing' activities can be encouraged. This in turn encourages peer and self-correction. Students can save a copy of their draft to a common area of the local area network accessible to the teacher and/or the group. Feedback can be given, with suggestions for improvement, and students can then share the redrafting process.

When word processing and e-mail are combined, as in writing to a partner school, the purpose of the activity and its audience become even clearer.

Students frequently enjoy producing brochures and display work. Word processing or desktop publishing using images and/or clip art can enable them to produce work of an almost professional quality. Images and clip art can easily be retrieved from the Internet to contextualise the work. My own students greatly enjoyed a unit of work based on geographical surroundings. The end point of the unit was the production of a brochure about their home town, intended for foreign visitors. Preparatory work included viewing in the ICT suite web sites of towns in a foreign country, alongside the classroom-based activities of acquisition of vocabulary and grammar in a typical context. Over three weeks, Listening, Speaking and Reading/Writing activities focused on the acquisition of the necessary language. Students were then given the opportunity during a lesson to view two different web sites of French towns, and asked to note presentation details, layout and the way language was used. Initial drafts of the texts were made and pupils worked on them in pairs. Feedback was given by peers and myself, and a lesson (1 hour 20 minutes) was given over to the production of the brochure. Finally, a display of the brochures was made on the wall outside the classroom. One of the benefits of such a unit of work was the pleasingly high levels of motivation in the group. Some of the best work produced came from students who do not always produce high-quality written work. For students with more advanced ICT skills, this activity could easily be extended to allow them to produce their own web sites, hosted on the school network Language area, or even live on the Internet.

## Teacher activity 8.1

- Consider your own teaching situation and explore the possibilities offered by your ICT facilities. Evaluate their potential and any limitations to their use.
- Assess your own needs in terms of ICT. Do you feel competent? What do you think your training needs are, and how can they be provided for?
- If you have good ICT facilities, think of an ICT-based activity linked to your current teaching unit and which could not be done in the classroom without ICT.
- Draw up a list of instructions in the TL for use in ICT activities.

## ICT and the future

Technology is moving fast. At the time of writing, data projectors and interactive whiteboards are appearing in an increasing number of schools. Data projectors make whole-class teaching with ICT a very fruitful experience, and also provide opportunities for teacher and students to make presentations to the whole class using programmes such as Microsoft PowerPoint. Wireless technology is also becoming ubiquitous, allowing laptops and other portable devices such as personal digital assistants and tablet PCs to take their place in the classroom. This technology has great potential for teaching FL using ICT, as teachers will no longer have to take their class to the ICT suite with all the limitations this can impose. Instead, the computers can now come to the FL classroom when they are needed, providing maximum flexibility in their use.

## ICT as a means of professional development

In order to integrate ICT into our teaching programmes, many of us feel we may need a helping hand along the way. Local FL ICT-specific training may not be available, but, thanks to the Internet, it is possible for FL teachers to have access to some excellent training materials. The following web sites have been found most useful by teachers in training sessions and are dedicated to FL.

- **ICT4LT**, www.ict4lt.org
  One of the authors of the training modules of this authoritative web site describes it thus (Davies, G. 2002: 7):

  The ICT4LT website is the outcome of a project funded under the Socrates Programme of the European Commission . . . at present the ICT4LT materials are mainly used as an on-line reference library . . . [and they] form the basis of ICT awareness and training courses delivered in the traditional way in many educational institutions, and also in connection with regular in-service training courses for teachers.

  The modules include an introduction to new technologies, CALL and the Internet, integrating CALL into study programmes, multimedia and creating a web site – amongst others.
- **BECTA** (British Educational Communications and Technology Agency), www.becta.org.uk
  This site has many useful links to language-related resources. For example, within the Community Languages section, the *Say IT* information sheet provides a range of common ICT terms and computer-related phrases in many languages.

- **ALL** (Association for Language Learning), www.all-languages.org.uk
- **CILT** (National Centre for Languages), www.cilt.org.uk
  This site's home page has a link to ICT. This in turn links to Lingu@NET UK, which has an extremely useful link, Websites for Languages, with many topic-grouped web sites in several languages. (To access the latter resources, click on the blue button, not the Linguanet Europa link on the Lingu@NET home page.)

Further useful web sites for FL teachers include these:

- BBC Languages, www.bbc.co.uk/languages
  This site has, on each language-specific area, a link to BBC Bitesize revision, which my own students have frequently used.
- Graham's Favourite Websites,
  www.camsoftpartners.co.uk/websites.htm
  This is a most comprehensive list of web sites for FL teachers.
- Learn.co.uk, www.learn.co.uk
  At present the free online exercises for students and resources exist in French only.

   This list is deliberately short. If you are seeking language-specific web sites, it is best to go to the CILT site and start your search there.

### Discussion groups
Many organisations such as CILT host discussion groups. CIE runs online training sessions and linked discussion groups in many subjects. Details of such ICT-based training opportunities can be accessed at CIE online, www.cie.org.uk

### LOOKING BACK

- ◆ What do you feel to be the potential of ICT in the FL context?
- ◆ If you have technical support staff in school, how could you best involve them in helping you to set up links to web sites you wish to access on a regular basis?
- ◆ How could information retrieval and e-mail enrich the learning environment of your situation?
- ◆ What advantages does word processing present to students? What have you learnt about 'flexible' text?

Bachman, L. F. (1990). *Fundamental Considerations in Language Testing.* Oxford: Oxford University Press.

Brumfit, C. (1984). *Communicative Methodology in Language Teaching: the Roles of Fluency and Accuracy.* Cambridge: Cambridge University Press.

Cajkler, W. and Addelman, R. (2000). *The Practice of Foreign Language Teaching* (repr. 2001, 2002). London: David Fulton Publishers.

Davies, A. (ed.) (1968). *Language Testing Symposium: a Psycholinguistic Perspective.* London: Oxford University Press.

Davies, G. (2002). www.ict4lt.org

Davies, G. (2003). 'ICT and Modern Foreign Languages: Learning Opportunities and Training Needs'. *Scottish Languages Review*, 8 June 2003.

European Language Network. www.icc-europe.com (report on ICT in Foreign Language learning).

Harrison, A. (1983). 'Communicative Testing: Jam Tomorrow?'. In A. Hughes and D. Porter (eds.), *Current Developments in Language Testing.* London: Academic Press.

Hedge, T. (1998). (Also 1988 edition.)*Writing.* Oxford: Oxford University Press.

Hedge, T. (2000). *Teaching and Learning in the Language Classroom.* Oxford: Oxford University Press.

Hewer, S. (1992). *Making the Most of IT Skills.* London: CILT.

Hymes, D. (1972). 'On Communicative Competence'. In J. B. Pride and J. Holmes (eds.), *Sociolinguistics.* Harmondsworth: Penguin Books.

Jones, C. (1986). ' "It's not so much the programme, more what you do with it": the Importance of Methodology in CALL'. *System*, vol. 14, no. 2.

Lussier, D. (1993). 'Evaluation et approche communicative'. In *Recherches et applications du français dans le monde. Numéro spécial. Evaluation et certifications en langue étrangère.* Paris: Hachette.

Macaro, E. (1997). *Target Language, Collaborative Learning and Autonomy.* Cleveland, Ohio: Multilingual Matters Ltd.

Macaro, E. (2000). 'Issues in Target Language Teaching'. In K. Field (ed.), *Issues in Modern Foreign Language Teaching.* London: Routledge.

MacDonald, C. (1993). *Using the Target Language.* Cheltenham: Mary Glasgow Publications.

Nunan, D. and Lamb, C. (1995). *The Self-Directed Teacher*. Cambridge: Cambridge University Press.

Pachler, N. and Field, K. (2002). *Learning to Teach Modern Foreign Languages in the Secondary School.* London: Routledge.

Richards, J. C. (1990). *The Language Teaching Matrix.* Cambridge: Cambridge University Press.

Scrivener, J. (1994). *Learning Teaching.* Oxford: Heinemann.

Silliman, E. R. and Wilkinson, L. C. (1991). *Communicating for Learning: Classroom Observation and Collaboration.* Gaithersburg, Maryland: Aspen.

Townsend, K. (1997). *Email – Using Electronic Communication in Foreign Language Teaching.* London: CILT.

Ur, P. (1981). *Discussions that Work.* Cambridge: Cambridge University Press.

Weir, C. J. (1988). *Communicative Language Testing.* Exeter: University of Exeter Press.

Weir, C. and Roberts, J. (1994). *Evaluation in ELT.* Oxford: Blackwell.

Woods, C. (1993). *Testing in the Target Language.* Unpublished MPhil. thesis, University of Exeter.

# Appendix B: glossary

| | |
|---|---|
| **activity** | a classroom activity helps learners achieve the lesson aims (e.g. a role-play activity may help to improve fluency) |
| **aim** | long-term target |
| **assessment** | collection of information concerning a learner's achievements and proficiency |
| **assessment objectives** | sets of skills students should develop, assessed in the final examinations to see how far they have been developed |
| **bottom-up processing** | understanding text by putting together information from phonological, lexical, grammatical and discoursal parts |
| **CALL** | Computer Assisted Language Learning |
| **CLT** | Communicative Language Teaching |
| **communicative language teaching** | where the teaching and learning goal is competence in language communication |
| **curriculum** | aims, methods, techniques and evaluation processes of a subject |
| **differentiation** | planned process of intervention in the classroom to maximise potential, based on individual student needs |
| **extensive reading** | reading in some quantity, to broaden effective and efficient reading habits and to increase range of vocabulary and structure |
| **follow-up activities** | activities used by a teacher to consolidate or extend learners' use of language |
| **formative assessment** | assessment of learners that assists the learning process, an assessment of current status and progress; usually relates closely to what is taught in the classroom |
| **gist** | main ideas without detail |
| **goals** | long-term aims, described in general terms |
| **ICT** | Information and Communication Technology |
| **integrating skills** | use of more than one language skill at the same time |
| **intensive reading** | usually requires detailed understanding of a text |
| **key word** | identifying key words in questions is a useful learner strategy for identifying those words that may lead to answers in a text |

| | |
|---|---|
| **language proficiency** | ability of a learner to use the Target Language for communication |
| **language skills** | learner's abilities in using a language – Reading and Listening (receptive) and Speaking and Writing (productive) |
| **language subskills** | divisions of skills (e.g. in Reading different strategies used depending on purpose and type of text) |
| **learner-centred approach** | teaching approach that focuses on and considers learners' needs and expectations |
| **lesson aims** | things learners should be able to do, or language they should be able to use, by the end of the lesson that they could not do or use at the start |
| **objective** | short-term target |
| **productive skills** | active skills: Speaking and Writing |
| **purpose** | reason for Speaking or Writing |
| **receptive skills** | passive skills: Reading and Listening |
| **register** | variations in a person's speech or writing depending on their purpose and audience |
| **reliability** | extent to which a test measures consistently |
| **scanning and skimming** | subskills of Reading which involve speed reading: with scanning, to find specific facts or details; with skimming, to obtain an overall idea of text content |
| **style** | see 'register' |
| **summative assessment** | assessment, usually at end of school term, year or longer course of study; may not relate directly to what is taught in the classroom |
| **task-based approach** | using tasks rather than vocabulary and grammar as the basis for a syllabus; these provide a real purpose in using language |
| **TL** | Target Language – the Foreign Language in which the student is expected to gain proficiency |
| **top-down processing** | understanding text by appraising what ought to be there, using background knowledge |
| **validity** | extent to which a test measures what it claims |

# Index

assessment 2, 6–7
assessment objectives 5, 88
authenticity, of tasks and text 15–16

classroom management, during
    speaking activities 44–5
collaborative writing 75–6
communicative language ability 12, 13
communicative language teaching 14
competence in languages 12
conversations
    general 52, 54–6
    topic 51, 54–6
core listening skills 33–4
core reading skills 68–9
core writing objectives 78
curriculum content, of FL syllabus 7

data projectors 85
*Defined Content* booklets 7, 8
discipline 23
discussion groups 86
discussions 46, 47–8
displays 23

e-mail, in FL teaching 82
evaluation, of students' work 27
extended listening skills 35
extended reading skills 69–70
extended writing skills 78–9
external examinations 2

fluency 13
foreign languages, reasons for
    learning 3–4
formative assessment 25–6, 28, 89
free reading 66–7

general conversations 46, 52
    marking 54–6
grammar 14
group discussions 47–8

ICT
    in FL teaching 80–6
    as means of professional
        development 85–6
    overview of 80–1

information retrieval 81–2
information-gap activities 47

learning objectives 27
lesson plans 10
lessons
    links between phases of 21
    using time constructively 20–1
listening activities, increasing students'
    participation in 35–6
listening resources 36–8
listening skills 29–40
    bottom-up 30, 32
    improving 31–2
    learning more effective 32–3
    participatory activities checklist 38–9
    top-down 30, 32–3
listening tests, observations of students
    during 29–30

mark scheme, for speaking tests 52–3
marking, of written work 27, 75, 76–7
methodology 12–14
mother tongues, teaching students
    with a variety of 23–4

oral work, correcting in TL 21

performance in languages 12
post-reading tasks 65
pre-reading tasks 63, 65
presentation – practice –
    communication language teaching
    model 41, 43
presentations 46, 51
profile sheets 27–8

question banks 48, 57–8
questions, hierarchy of 58–9

reading activities 64–5
reading comprehension skills 62–3
reading corner 66–7
reading skills 62–70
    bottom-up 63
    top-down 63
reading subskills 64
reading tasks 63, 65